Vested in Christ

Printed in China

Publisher's Cataloging-In-Publication Data

Names: Danias, George, author. | Hatzithanasi-Danias, Christina, author. | Haztithanasi-Antonatou, Paraskevi, illustrator. | Monos, Michael, translator.

Title: Vested in Christ : understanding the mystery of Holy Baptism and sacred Chrismation / George Danias & Christina Hatzithanasi-Danias ; with illustrations by Paraskevi Haztithanasi-Antonatou ; [translated by the Rev. Fr. Michael Monos].

Other Titles: Chrēston enedysasthe. English

Description: [First English edition]. | Columbia, Missouri : Newrome Press, 2019. | First Greek edition: Athens, Greece : Athos E.P.E., an imprint of Stamoulis A.E, 2016.

Identifiers: ISBN 9781939028785

Subjects: LCSH: Baptism (Liturgy) | Chrismation--Liturgy. | Orthodox Eastern Church--Liturgy.

Classification: LCC BX378.B3 D3613 2019 | DDC 264.019081--dc23

GEORGE DANIAS & CHRISTINA HATZITHANASI-DANIAS

with Illustrations by Paraskevi Haztithanasi-Antonatou

Vested in Christ

Understanding the Mysteries of Holy Baptism and Sacred Chrismation

Newrome

PRESS

COLUMBIA, MISSOURI

2019

Dedicated

*to our Parents who brought us into the world,
and to our Godparents for our rebirth in Christ,
and to our Spiritual Fathers for the restoration
of the brilliance of our baptismal garment.*

CONTENTS

INTRODUCTION

PRAYERS AFTER BIRTH

PART ONE

Preparation for Holy Baptism

PART TWO
Holy Baptism

PART THREE
Post Baptismal Prayers

Prologue to the Greek Edition

oly Baptism is the Mystery during which a person is born again and recreated; the image of God within is restored, formerly shattered by Adam and Eve's disobedience in the Garden of Paradise. St. Paul emphasizes the significance of the Mystery of Holy Baptism: *For as many of you as have been baptized into Christ have put on Christ.* (Gal. 3: 27) This means that at Holy Baptism, we put on Christ, and at Sacred Christmation, we receive the enlightenment of the Holy Spirit!

When St. Synclitike (commemorated Jan. 5) was persuaded by the syncretists to explain the benefit of Holy Baptism, she said to them: "In the present life we are born three times: The first time, when we go forth from our mother's womb, coming from the earth to the earth. The other two times we are born, we rise from the earth to heaven. Of these two second births, one is brought about by divine Grace at Holy Baptism and is rightly called rebirth and regeneration. The other is also brought about by divine Grace, when we repent..."

The saints interpreted the Mystery of Holy Baptism as a revelation of the measure of the love of Christ for mankind. It was this divine Love, which we ourselves have experienced, that urged us to author the present book. Indeed, it was sufficient to motivate us to offer this effort to everyone who has been baptized!

We developed the present book according to the order of the Service of Holy Baptism, as it is described in the Euchologion of our Church–recognizing that it is entirely possible to encounter examples of small alterations to the order of the celebration of the rite which do not affect the essence of the Mystery. The drawings in the book and the juxtaposition of the narratives from the Book of Elders and Lives of the Saints (Gerontiko and Synaxaria), are intended to assist the untaught in approaching this sacred Mystery.

The book *Holy Baptism* by Hieromonk Gregorios served as the basic foundation for the present book. It can serve as a kind of source book for those who wish to find the references to the Patristic and iconographic citations mentioned in this book, but, which have been eliminated for brevity and simplicity, as this book is primarily intended for young people. We want to give special thanks to Geronta Gregorios and the brotherhood of the Cell of St. John the Theologian, Koutloumousiou Monastery, Mount Athos, for their invaluable assistance. We also would like to thank artist Paraskevi Hatzithanasi for her illustrations, which adorn this book. Additionally, we would like to extend our appreciation to all those who contributed, in one way or another, to this undertaking.

Furthermore, we wholeheartedly pray that every Christian endeavors to make the baptismal garment he received on the day of his baptism even brighter. Finally, we pray that the multitude of divine gifts received at Holy Baptism, which transcend human thought, extended to more and more people!

George and Christina Danias

Prologue to the English Edition

Baptism in Christ is a natural consequence of faith in Christ. Through Holy Baptism, those who have believed in Christ and accepted Him as their Savior are given the possibility to become children of God. As St. John Chrysostom writes, "the magnitude of God's gifts [bestowed by Holy Baptism] defies human description." (Catechetical Instruction 4)

Nevertheless, our Lord's commandment to His Disciples, following the Resurrection, *Go [therefore] and make disciples of all nations, baptizing them in the Name of the Father and of the Son and of the Holy Spirit,* (Mt. 28:19) urged us to write *Vested in Christ.* We offer it as a small contribution towards a better understanding of the gifts of baptismal Grace. The English translation of this book by Fr. Michael Monos and Newrome Press, is a continuation of this effort.

It is our prayer that, with the assistance of this book, people everywhere will come to know and love our Lord, and receive Holy Baptism. And may all of us, who have already received Holy Baptism, preserve our baptismal garment undefiled so that together we may enter *into the splendor of His holy ones.* (Ps. 109:3)

George and Christina Danias

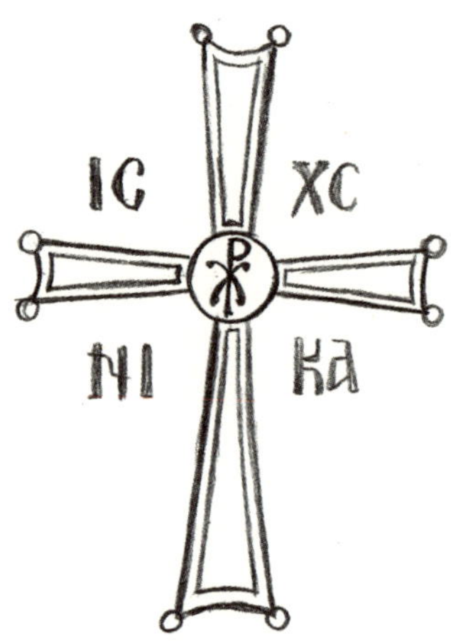
IC XC
NI KA

INTRODUCTION

The Sacred Mysteries

The Mysteries are divinely established rites of our Church which transmit invisible divine Grace to the faithful through perceptible signs. They are called Mysteries (from the root *μύω* [mē-oh] which means to shut one's eyes or mouth) for two reasons. Firstly, because they are not comprehensible to human reason, and secondly, because unbelievers are not permitted to attend them. From the 13th century onwards, it has been generally held that there are seven Holy Mysteries, according to the seven gifts of the Holy Spirit (Is. 11:1–2). The Mysteries are: Holy Baptism, Sacred Chrismation, the Divine Eucharist, Confession, Holy Orders, Marriage, and Holy Oil.

The Mysteries have a dual character—visible and invisible, perceptible and imperceptible—because the human person who participates in them has both thought and sense-perception. The invisible element is the divine Grace of the Holy Spirit, which in various ways, sanctifies the souls and bodies of the faithful. The perceptible element in each of the Divine Mysteries is various, for example wine, oil, water, etc.

The rites of the Holy Mysteries comprise all the gifts of the Holy Spirit for Christians. In order to receive divine sanctifying Grace through these rites, the faithful must co-operate with God. A valid Holy Mystery requires that it be celebrated by a Bishop or Presbyter who has been canonically* ordained.

All of the Mysteries have been transmitted to us by Christ in word and deed. He participated in all of them Himself, not out of need, but rather to show us the road to salvation.

First, above all, He received Holy Baptism when He was baptized by the Honorable Forerunner in the Jordan River, and Holy Christmation when the Holy Spirit descended upon Him in the form of a dove. The Lord taught His Disciples that these Mysteries were to be celebrated in succession when He sent them to baptize the nations *in the Name of the Father and the Son and the Holy Spirit.* (Mt. 28:19)

Christ officiated the Mystery of the Divine Eucharist during the Mystical Supper, and taught His Disciples with the command: *Do this in memory of Me.* (Lk. 22:19)

---

* Blue highlighted words are defined in the Glossary on p. 157

The Lord Himself also taught the Mystery of Confession to the Apostles when He gave them authority to forgive sins saying, *If you forgive anyone's sins, they are forgiven.* (Jn. 20:23)

Likewise, He received the Mystery of the Priesthood at His Transfiguration when His heavenly Father proclaimed, *This is My beloved Son in Whom I am well-pleased. Listen to Him!* (Mt. 17:5) and gave witness through the Holy Spirit that Christ is our Teacher, Shepherd and High-Priest. Christ then gave the Priesthood to the Disciples calling them Apostles (messengers), and sent them to teach the nations. (Mt. 28:20)

The Lord Himself also blessed honorable Marriage at Cana in Galilee (Jn. 2:1–11), and He became the Bridegroom of the Church. (Mt. 27:27–31)

Finally, He established the Mystery of Holy Oil when He commanded the Disciples to anoint the sick with oil and to heal them. (Mk. 6:13)

The Lord's descent to earth opened a road for mankind that leads to heaven. Following His Ascension, He left that road open—the road of the Divine Mysteries! In this book, we will discuss the first Mystery, which is Holy Baptism. It is this Mystery which introduces us to the Christian life.

THE SPIRIT OF GOD
HOVERED UPON THE WATERS

Foreshadowings of Holy Baptism

The life of mankind before the Fall was angelic. God created all things for man's benefit. Man was made indestructible and immortal—spared from all concerns of the body—and God placed him in the Garden of Paradise. He had no need for clothing, since he was clothed with divine glory—God wanted His beloved creature to live in the Garden as an earthly Angel!

Mankind lost this bright and beautiful raiment when our first parents, Adam and Eve, disobeyed the divine command in the Garden of Eden. And what had been a life of constant divine joy became one of loss, struggle, and death.

However, the benevolent God did not abandon mankind in his sin! During the entire age of the Old Testament, mankind was being prepared to receive the gift of Grace. All of the personages and events of this era prophesied Christ and foreshadowed His incarnation, the coming era of Grace.

THE SALVATION OF NOAH THROUGH THE ARK

Thus, the Mystery of Holy Baptism was foreshadowed by many events in the Old Testament. St. Gregory of Nyssa explains that, "the form of Holy Baptism was not clearly revealed, but the benevolent God foreshadowed it allegorically." In other words, God was giving hints of what was to come when the Messiah would appear.

We encounter the first foreshadowing of Holy Baptism in the Book of Genesis in the story of the creation of the world. We read that the Spirit of God hovered above the waters. This prefigured what would happen in the new creation, when mankind would be reborn by water and Spirit at Holy Baptism.

The second event which foreshows Holy Baptism is the Great Flood. The salvation of Noah and his family in the ark was a pattern of the salvation of mankind in our holy Church by water and Spirit.

CROSSING THE RED SEA

Yet another prefigurement—from a catalog of many wondrous events of the Old Testament which foreshadow Holy Baptism—was the crossing of the Red Sea by the Hebrew people. In the Book of Exodus, we read how God directed Moses to raise his staff at shore of the Red Sea. Immediately, the waters were separated, leaving a path through which Israelites might pass. The illumined cloud, which the people had been following up to that point in time, now moved between God's chosen people and the pursuing Egyptian army. St. Gregory Palamas explains that the sea is a prototype for "the water of Holy Baptism," since "the cloud foretells of the overshadowing presence of the Holy Spirit upon those who are baptized."

Circumcision, which the Israelites performed on male children on the eighth day after birth, was also a prototype of Holy Baptism. St. John Damascene explains, that "for the Israelites, fleshly circumcision served until the great circumcision came, that is, Holy Baptism, which circumcises us from sin, and seals us with the name of God."

Finally, Judaic baptism constitutes yet another prototype of Christian Baptism. St. John Chrysostom mentions that it "cleansed bodily impurities, but not sins of conscience." It was a symbolic practice that God decreed for the Jews of the Old Testament, and which symbolized the purification that would later be offered by Christian Baptism.

The Baptism of St. John the Forerunner

The connecting link between the Old and New Testaments is St. John the Baptist. When the Forerunner preached to the Jews, he admonished them: *Therefore, bring forth fruit worthy of repentance!* (Mt. 3:8) This was an invitation to purify the inner self by means of repentance, in order to receive the Lord. St. Cyril of Alexandria writes that Holy Scripture calls the time before the bodily Incarnation of Jesus Christ on earth the *night*, while it calls His presence on earth the *day*. In between the dark of the night and the light of the day, we find the Honorable Forerunner. He is the *dawn* who announces the coming *day* of the Lord.

It is precisely for this reason that John the Baptist was the Forerunner of the Savior. Likewise, the baptism that he performed was a forerunner of the saving Baptism of Christ. This means that the baptism of John was superior to the Judaic one, but inferior to ours since it did not impart the gift of the Holy Spirit, nor did it grant divine Grace which is the forgiveness of sin. The Baptist urged a change of heart, but he did not have the authority to offer forgiveness. This is, indeed, why he said, *I indeed baptize you in water for repentance...He will baptize you in the Holy Spirit and with fire.* (Mt 3:11)

The Honorable Forerunner baptized those who came to Him with water, and at the moment of their baptism, they confessed their sins. Afterwards, he led them to Christ, who later would baptize them with the fire of the grace of the Holy Spirit. St. Basil the Great thus summarizes, "the baptism of John was an introduction, whereas the baptism of Christ was perfection. St. John's was the cutting off from sin, by which a person comes to know God."

The Baptism of Christ

The Baptism of the Lord in the Jordan is the constitutive act of the Mystery itself. As the Mystical Supper was the beginning of the Mystery of the Divine Eucharist, likewise the baptism of Christ by the Honorable Forerunner was the beginning of the Mystery of Holy Baptism.

We read in the Gospel of Matthew (3:13-17):

Then Jesus came from Galilee to the Jordan to be baptized by John. However, John would have prevented Him, saying, "I need to be baptized by You, and [it is] You who come to me?"

But Jesus answered and said to him, "Allow it for now, for it is fitting that in this way, we should fulfill all righteousness." Then John allowed Jesus [to be baptized].

THE BAPTISM
ΙΩ
ΙC XC
Ο Ν

After He had been baptized, Jesus immediately came out of the water and behold, the heavens were opened to Him. He saw the Spirit of God descending as a dove and coming down on Him. And behold, a voice from heaven said:

"This is My beloved Son, with Whom I am well pleased!

When Christ asked St. John to baptize Him, the Baptist prevented Him saying: *I need to be baptized by You, and [it is] You who come to me?* And Christ responded, *Allow it for now, for it is fitting that in this way, we should fulfill all righteousness.*

Did Christ need to be baptized? No, Christ did not require Holy Baptism. Nevertheless, the benevolent Lord established this path for our salvation. St. John Chrysostom explains that, "it is like what happened at Pascha. Christ celebrated it twice. First, the Judaic Passover came to an end, and the Christian Pascha was inaugurated. At His Baptism, He discharged the Judaic tradition, and at the same time, He also opened the gates of the Baptism of the Church."

The Baptism of Christ "by the prophet John was a sign of the old [Covenant]. The descent of the Holy Spirit verified the new Grace. Christ did the same thing as a Person who stands between the two things that are separated by some distance and connects them with His outspread hands: He united the Old with the New, the divine with human nature, the things that were His with the things that are ours." This union of heaven and earth was revealed at the Baptism of Christ when the heavens were opened.

St. Gregory Palamas explains why the heavens opened at the Lord's Baptism, saying, "Do you see that Holy Baptism is the Heavenly Gate that every baptized person enters? Everything that happened to Christ occurred for our benefit. It follows, then, that Christ opened the heavens for us, and having opened the Heavenly Gates, they anticipate our entrance."

Similarly, St. John Chrysostom says that, "at our Baptism, Christ sends the Holy Spirit, who invites us into the heavenly fatherland. He does not make us Angels or Archangels, but elects us to be sons of God!"

Prayers after Birth

1. The Prayers on the first day of the life of a child

The birth of a human person is a festive, resurrectional joy. St. John Chrysostom writes that the birth of children "are a very great consolation for death which comes with the disobedience of Adam and Eve. It is for this reason that God...grants the birth of offspring, revealing in a sense an image of resurrection." From the very first day of life, our Holy Mother, the Church, participates in this joyful foretaste of the resurrection!

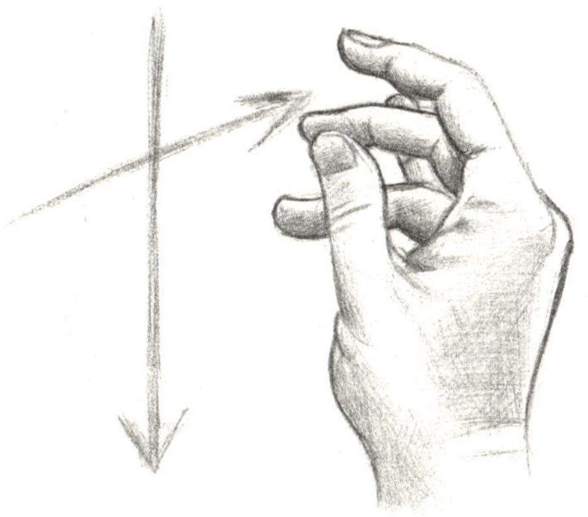

It is for this reason that, as soon as a child is born, a Priest is called to the birthplace. There, in the presence of the newly born infant and the child's mother, he reads the appointed prayers. These prayers doxologize the Lord, and thank Him for a new life that has been born into the world. The Priest blesses the infant with the sign of the Cross and asks God to make the child worthy of Holy Baptism.

2. Prayers on the Eighth Day—Naming

The naming of a child is celebrated on the eighth day after birth; the infant is also again sealed with the sign of the life-creating Cross. This service is appointed for the eighth day following the pattern of our Lord. On that day, according to the ancient Judaic practice, He was circumcised and received His name, Jesus.

Amongst the words of the prayer that the Priest prays: ... that the light of Your face may be signed upon Your servant *N.*, and place the sign of the Cross of Your only-begotten Son in *his / her* heart and thoughts...saying this, the Priest seals the forehead and chest of the infant.

The first name that a person receives in preparation for Holy Baptism is *servant of the Lord, Christian.* Christian means: a person of Christ, a person who is descended from Christ. For this reason, St. John Chrysostom exhorts us, "Understand that to be named after Christ is of inestimable value! Therefore, we must not do things that dishonor the name that we have received...Rather, let us perceive and honor the magnificence of our naming." And St. Ignatios the God-bearer complements this, saying, "We must not only be called Christians, but be Christians!"

It is during this prayer that the Priest proclaims the name which the parent's have chosen for the child. St. John Chrysostom encourages us "...not to give our children ordinary names...but names of holy people who have excelled in virtue, and who have great boldness before the Lord." In this way, the person will share his name with a fervent intercessor, and whose manner of life he can reliably imitate.

During the naming service, the Church prescribes that the infant be sealed with the sign of the life-creating Cross. As is well known, historically, a brand was used to mark the belongings—including livestock—and lands of an estate holder. The life-creating Cross is the brand with which our Lord and Good Shepherd marks us!

In the Old Testament, the Israelites practiced male circumcision on the eighth day. This ancient practice foreshadowed sealing with the life-creating Cross. At that time, circumcision was given as a sign used to separate the Israelites from other people. "They were physically marked by circumcision," writes St. John Chrysostom, "and they also branded their livestock and horses. We are branded, however, as sons and daughters, by the Holy Spirit." The faithful are able to recognize one another with this sign. St. Basil the Great writes that the holy Angels recognize the faithful by the sign of Cross!

3. Prayers on the Fortieth Day —Churching

The next pre-baptismal rite—Churching (also called the Forty Day Blessing)—is celebrated 40 days after birth. Churching follows the example of Christ's entry into the Temple 40 days after His birth, in accordance with Mosaic Law. On that day, the Lord was brought to the Temple by His all-Holy Mother and Joseph, and received into the arms of the elder Symeon. We celebrate this feast—the Presentation of the Lord—on February 2nd.

The deeper meaning of the rite is the dedication of a human person to God—even before he takes his first steps! The child's mother comes to the Lord's Temple, and dedicates her child to our common mother, the holy Church. She beseeches the Lord: Bless that what You have entrusted to me!

Before the completion of the rite of Churching, the Priest takes the infant in his arms, and there, at the entryway to the Church, he makes the sign of the Cross over the body of the child saying: The servant of God *N.* is Churched in the

THE PRESENTATION

FORTY DAY BLESSING OF THE CHILD

name of the Father, and the Son, and the Holy Spirit. He then enters the Church; that is, into the earthly palace of Christ's Kingdom.

The rite of Churching prepares a person for his approaching Baptism. As the Cross opened Paradise, so too does the Cross take the human race by the hand and lead it into the Kingdom of the Heavens. In other words, the Cross becomes the Gate of Paradise for the newborn child.

By this liturgical act—the blessing of the child's body with the sign of the Cross—the Church teaches us that Holy Baptism crucifies the old man, obliterates sin, and makes his entrance into the heavenly Kingdom possible.

Based on what we have said about the prayers after birth, we can see that the Church embraces the newborn child from the very beginning of his life: **a)** on the first day the baby is blessed and is welcomed into the world; **b)** on the eighth day the infant is given a Christian name—previously selected by his parents—and that name is blessed; **c)** on the fortieth day the child is dedicated to God.

However, the infant does not yet fully belong to the Church, since he is not yet a member of the Body of Christ. At this point, he stands within the inner-courtyard of the lordly palaces, and is prepared to be led into the inner sanctum by the Mystery of Holy Baptism.

After the 40 day blessing, the Church waits in expectation to offer this person the Mysteries of Baptism, Chrismation and Holy Communion. At that time, he will be called a *son of God and inheritor of the Kingdom of Heaven.*

From the life of St. Philemon—celebrated on December 14—we read the following: St. Philemon was a former idol worshipper, who now stood before a certain ruler named Arrianos. He was about to be martyred for his faith in Christ when the ruler said to him, "You call yourself a Christian in vain! Even if you die for Christ, you will not be numbered among the martyrs, because you haven't been baptized." Hearing this Philemon responded:

"Thank you, sir! Your words have greatly benefited me—you have reminded me about the importance of Holy Baptism."

And then turning around towards the onlookers, he cried out:

"Please, if there is a Christian among you who is not afraid to die, come and baptize me!" However, no one came forward out of fear. Seeing this, St. Philemon, with tear-filled eyes, set his gaze on heaven and said:

"Christ, my Lord and Master, You have redeemed me from the idolater's trap. I beg you, do not leave me unbaptized. Send me some water, and a Priest who might baptize me."

THE BAPTISM OF ST. PHILEMON

Immediately after he said this, a wondrous raincloud descended from heaven and baptized Philemon. Then the cloud ascended and disappeared. St. Philemon turned towards his brother believers and said, "My fellow Christians, though no one had the courage to help me, it is obvious that the Master Christ Himself came and baptized me!"

Then, turning towards the ruler he added, "And you, sir, look how God prevented your futile rage against the Christians!"

Unrepentant, the ruler became even angrier! He ordered that the Saint be hung from a tree and for some archers to shoot him with their arrows. Some of the arrows pierced the tree, while others fell to the ground, and yet others miraculously floated in the air. As Arrianos was watching these amazing sights, a single arrow fell from the sky and stabbed him directly in the eye with such force that he was immediately blinded. But his blindness became a cause for the illumination of his soul!

Later, Arrianos was healed when dirt from St. Philemon's grave was applied to his eye. On account of this, he believed in Christ, and he and his entire company was baptized!

LET THE LITTLE CHILDREN COME TO ME...

Infant Baptism

The Evangelists relate an event that happened when the Lord *arrived at the borders of Judea, by the other side of the Jordan.* The inhabitants *brought little children to Him so that He might touch them, but the disciples rebuked those who were bringing them. But when Jesus saw this, He was indignant. He said to them, "Let the little children come to me and do not forbid them! For the Kingdom of God belongs to such as these...He took the children in His arms and blessed them, laying His hands on them.* Our holy Church has practiced infant Baptism from the very beginning, and this passage from Holy Scripture helps us understand why that is the case. Not only did the Lord bless the little children, but He commanded that they be allowed to come near Him! In the early Church, though infant Baptism did occur, oftentimes it was delayed until adulthood. The Apostolic Constitution advises: "Do you also baptize your infants, and bring them up in the nurture and admonition of God..."

As the years passed, infant Baptism slowly became the prevalent practice. The main reason for this was the danger of sudden death, since at that time the rate of infant mortality was much higher. According to St. Gregory the Theologian, "it is preferable that infants, though without cognition, be sanctified, rather than to depart this life unbaptized." Today, healthy babies typically receive the rites of baptism some time after the Forty Day Blessing. The exception are those cases when a baby is born ill. In such circumstances, the infant must be baptized sooner—even immediately after his birth (needful Baptism).

St. Kosmas the Aitolian speaks about emergency baptism in his teachings. "Brethren, it is preferable for 100 baptized people to perish than for one child to die unbaptized. And if perchance a child is expected to die, then it is not necessary to wait for a Priest to come and baptize the baby at the Church. Instead, whomever may be present can baptize the baby, whether father, mother, brother, neighbor or even the midwife. Take a sufficient amount of water and oil, make the sign of the Cross over the infant and baptize him saying: *The servant of God (Name) is baptized in the name of the Father, and the Son and the Holy Spirit. Amen.* If the child survives, a Priest should complete the rite. What should be done if you don't have any water? Take three handfuls of dirt and pour it on the baby's head and say the same as if you had water. But if you don't have dirt, what should be done? Baptize the baby in the air and say the very same thing."

From the life of the Venerable Arsenios the Cappadocian we learn the following: When the news of the exchange of populations reached Farasa, the Saint decided to baptize all the unbaptized children on account of the unpredictable dangers on the trip to Greece.

The Venerable Anastasios of Sinai narrates the following wondrous story:

When he was living in Laodicea of Syria, near Mt. Lebanon, opposite Gavthison, he heard about the following remarkable event from the elders there. There was, he said, a certain Presbyter in that place. One night, a man hurriedly came to him and asked him to get up and to baptize his infant child who was near death. The Presbyter got up from his bed and immediately began to perform the rite of Holy Baptism. However, as they prepared the water and the holy oil, and while the Presbyter continued the service, the child died unbaptized. The Presbyter then took the child and put him in front of the baptismal font and said, "Guardain Angel: you know well the power that Christ gave to His Priests—to bind and to loose in heaven and on earth. Therefore, I ask that you return the soul of this child back to his body until he is baptized, since you were not sent to take the unbaptized. We share the same Lord, and He knows that I have not acted negligently, but just awoke and immediately began the rite of Holy Baptism." The Presbyter spoke these words to the Angel and the child was resurrected, baptized, and then again fell asleep in the Lord."

Concerning the issue of infant Baptism, St. John Chrysostom says, "We baptize children, even though they are sinless, so that we can grant them sanctification, righteousness, divine sonship and inheritance, and to become a member of Christ and a dwelling place of the Holy Spirit." St. Gregory the Theologian urges parents to baptize their children in infancy: "Let's not act wrongly! Sanctify your child during infancy. Dedicate him to the Holy Spirit when he is young... Give him to the Holy Trinity, Who is the greatest and most excellent Protection."

Once, when St. Gregory the Theologian was traveling by boat from Alexandria to Greece, he found himself in danger of sinking. At the time he was unbaptized. His fellow travelers were afraid that they would suffer the same fate—a terrible death by drowning. "What a wretch! I was in danger, of dying unbaptized; I craved the spiritual water of Holy Baptism admist the deadly waters of the sea! So, I cried out to the Lord and begged Him to give me a little more time." Later, St. Gregory would urge those who had delayed receiving Holy Baptism: So long as you travel with fair weather, beware of shipwreck...Accept the gift of Holy Baptism joyfully, and not mournfully at death's door."

For all these reasons, our Church established the practice of infant Baptism. Holy Baptism is the first-fruit of divine gifts. When an infant is baptized, he is offered "beauty, honor, glory and dignities, which far exceed our worthiness."

Naturally, infant Baptism does not abolish the freedom of man. Whether the newly baptized remains an active member of the Church or will reject the gift of the Mystery is completely within his own power to decide. It is his choice alone whether or not he will follow the commandments of Christ. The gifts of the Holy Spirit, given during Holy Baptism, are only activated with the conscious participation of an individual in the life of the Church.

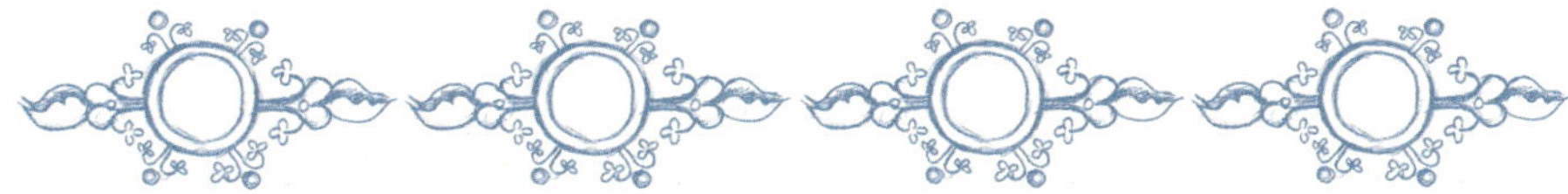

The Sponsor

In the early Church, it was customary for a person seeking entry into the catechumenate and Holy Baptism, to ask a Christian to present him to the Bishop of the local Church. This Christian was called the Sponsor. The Sponsor was responsible to speak on behalf of the good intentions of the candidate before the Church.

The Sponsor (or Godparent) guarantees the intentions and the future life of the Catechumen. He is the "guarantor in Christ that the Catechumen will keep the faith and live a Christian life."

For this reason, St. John Chrysostom encourages Sponsors, "We should not imagine that Sponsors have an ordinary relationship with their Godchild. You should well understand that, if by reason of their counsels they lead their Godchild on the road of virtue, they participate in their spiritual progress.

However, if they are indolent [in their responsibilities], their judgment will be severe. For this reason, it is a custom to call Sponsors Spiritual Fathers."

The Sponsor has a great responsibility to his Godchild. Christ, the Sponsor of the human race, offers the baptismal Sponsor great assistance. By the grace of Christ, the Sponsor becomes a co-worker in the mystery of the restoration of his Godchild's life and existence through the Mystery of Holy Baptism.

PART TWO
PREPARATION FOR HOLY BAPTISM

Prayer for the Making of a Catechumen

Before receiving Holy Baptism, a person is spiritually prepared by special prayers. A Priest, wearing his stole, turns the Catechumen towards the East and breaths on his face three times. Simultaneously, using his right hand, he seals the forehead and chest of the Catechumen three times with the sign of the Cross.

In the God-inspired book of Genesis it is written: *And God formed the man of dust of the earth and breathed upon his face the breath of life and the man became a living soul.* From the very beginning, breath was a sign of life. The Priest approaches the Catechumen and breathes on his face, because Baptism is the Mystery by which a person receives new life and is spiritually regenerated. St. Symeon of Thessaloniki explains that the Catechumen, "is breathed on three times, for the divine

activity of the life-creating Trinity. In the beginning, man was created by the Holy Trinity, and now at his Holy Baptism, he is recreated."

So, in the same way it happened at the creation of mankind in the beginning, it happens now: The Celebrant who serves as the mouth and hand of the Creator, blows the breath of life into the face of the one to be enlightened. And the candidate, by this act, receives "the Holy Spirit who gives life and creates and perfects and sanctifies all things."

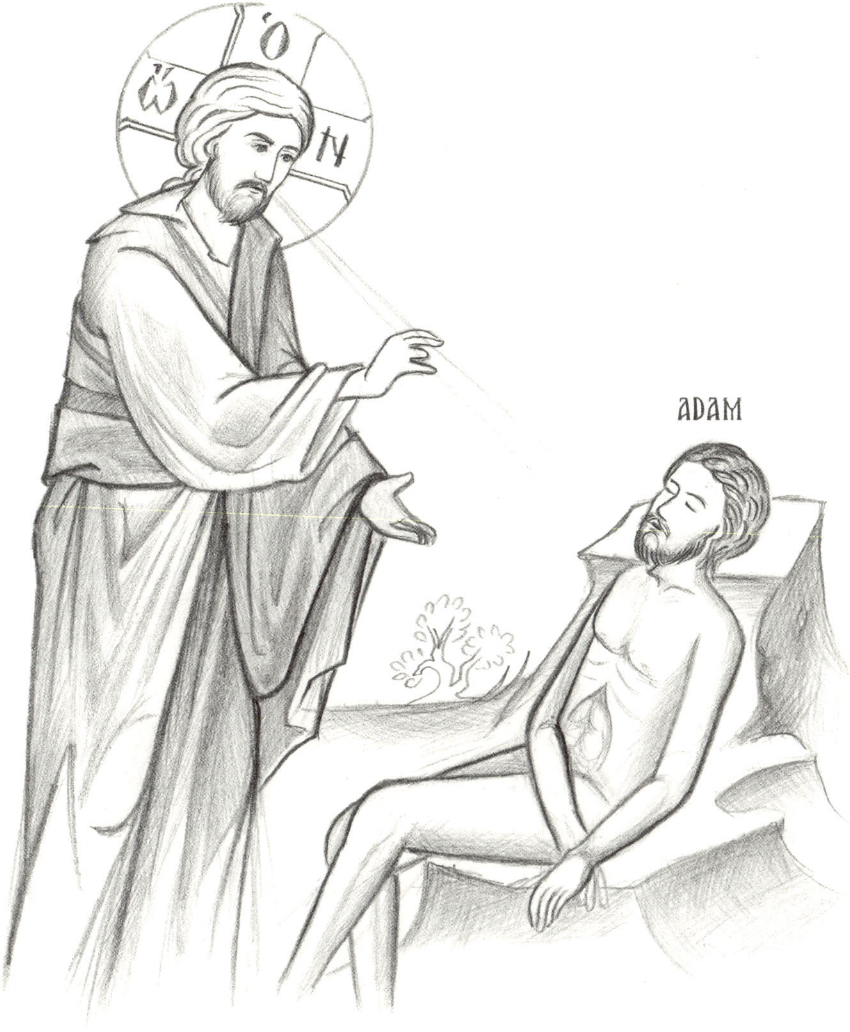

Continuing, the Priest touches the head of then Catechumen with his hand, and saying: Remove from *him / her* that ancient error, and fill *him / her* with faith in You, and hope and love, so that *he / she* may know that You alone are God, true God, and Your Only-Begotten Son, our Lord Jesus Christ, and Your Holy Spirit.

With these words, the Priest transmits the words of Christ to the **baptismal candidate**—the same thing the Lord said to Nikodemos: *Amen, amen, I tell you; unless one is born anew, he* *cannot see the Kingdom of God!* This means that someone who has not been baptized "neither has approached the threshold of the knowledge of the truth, nor even stands at the [monumental] entrance, but is wandering outside the Kingdom." For this reason, amongst the divine goods which a person enjoys when he is baptized is divine knowledge—to be honored to know God and to know well the truth.

A little later the Priest prays, ...That *he / she* may confess You, worshipping and glorifying Your great and most high Name, and may praise You throughout all the days of *his / her* life.

As previously stated, we know that at Holy Baptism we begin to love God. Since our Holy Church recognizes the great benefit received from doxologizing God, it prays for the candidate to doxologize the Name of the Lord for his entire life!

How does a person doxologize God? St. John Chrysostom answers, "Our eyes doxologize when they do not gaze on debauchery. Our tongue when it chants. Our ear when it does not listen to wicked music, nor accusations against a neighbor. The mind doxologizes when it does not scheme but overflows with love. Our feet, when not running to do evil deeds, but taking care to do good deeds. Our hands, when not tearing apart or grabbing more and more material goods or injuring a brother, but showing mercy and sheltering the aggrieved. In this way, a person becomes a well-tuned instrument which offers God a spiritual melody and a unified voice...If we continually doxologize God in this way, we will pass the present life without difficulties and will enjoy future divine benefits."

Exorcism

As the preparation for Holy Baptism continues, the Priest reads the first exorcism: The Lord rebukes you, O Devil, the Lord Who came into the world and dwelt among mankind so that He might destroy your tyranny...

Before a person believes in Christ, his heart "is a dwelling place of demons, because it acts in opposition to God's will." For this reason, the Church reads the prayers of exorcism for those who have prepared to be baptized. These prayers entreat Christ to expel any demons present in a person, so that the baptismal candidate becomes a ready dwelling place for God.

An additional reason that the prayers of exorcism are read is to break any bond of influence that the Devil holds over an individual, including infants. St. Symeon of Thessaloniki says the Priest has an obligation to read these prayers carefully, as

with all sacred prayers, saying them slowly so that they can heard by everyone present.

The prayers of exorcism have their origin in one of the Lord's miracles: the liberation of the demoniac from the Devil's tyranny. The Lord rebuked the demons with the order, *I command you, come out of him, and never enter him again!* The Church liberates the baptismal candidate from the tryanny of the Devil by invoking the name of Christ: Be afraid, come out, withdraw from this creature...Come out, and withdraw from the sealed and newly-enlisted soldier of Christ our God...Come out, and withdraw from this creature with all Your power and Your angels.

Thus, with the prayers of exorcism, our Holy Church invokes the power and love of God, and in the name of divine Love, commands the Devil to depart from the person preparing to be baptized.

The second prayer of exorcism mentions the wondrous works which God has done, beginning with the creation of the world, and continues to do until the second all-glorious coming of Christ to earth. Amongst them, the Priest mentions the crossing of the Red Sea by the Hebrews: Fear God, at whose command the earth was established upon the waters, Who created the heavens and fixed the mountains with a king post and the valleys with a cross-beam, placed sand as a boundary for the sea, and made a safe path through wild water.

The crossing of the Red Sea (Fear God...[who]...made a safe path through wild water) is one of the events that prefigures Holy Baptism. St. John Chrysostom compares the liberation of the Hebrews from the tyranny of Pharaoh with Holy Baptism, saying, "There the Hebrews were spared from the Egyptians by the sea. There in Holy Baptism we are spared from idolatry. There Pharaoh was drowned, while here the Devil is drowned. The Hebrews were spared from enslavement to the Egyptians, whereas we are saved from enslavement to the demons. The Hebrews marched to freedom, while we also do the same, but not to the same sort of liberation, but rather to one infinitely more brilliant!"

After he reads the third prayer of exorcism, the Priest prays and entreats the Lord for the person who is proceeding to Baptism: Yoke to *his / her* life an Angel of light, to deliver *him / her* from every attack of the Adversary, from evil encounter, from the noon-day demon, and from evil visions.

In this prayer, the Celebrant beseeches God to send the candidate an Angel of Light. The person who draws near to the holy baptismal font is given "an Angelic protector who will always be with the baptized person in order to expel the envious demons and ever-present temptation of the cunning enemy. He will lead him into the Kingdom of the Heavens, it is enough that the baptized person maintain in faith and deed the grace of Holy Baptism from defilement." We must take great care concerning this last point, because sin causes this angelic protection to withdraw and makes us again servants of the demons.

In the sayings of St. Makarios the Egyptian, it mentions the following incident: "Abba Makarios said: When I came to Constantinople and was walking around the city, I saw—with noetic sight—a person sitting outside a brothel, crushed with regret, his face in his hands, weeping...I approached him and said: Why are you weeping so sorrowfully? Why don't you leave this place? This is the den of prostitutes and licentious women. And he answered me: I am an Angel, an all-glorious servant of God. At the time of Baptism, every Christian receives an Angel from God. I am one of these Angels, and the person whom I am supposed to guard and protect is inside this brothel. Seeing him do iniquitous and licentious deeds, I am grieved; that's why you found me sitting here...How can I not weep [to see] the image of God falling into such darkness? I said to

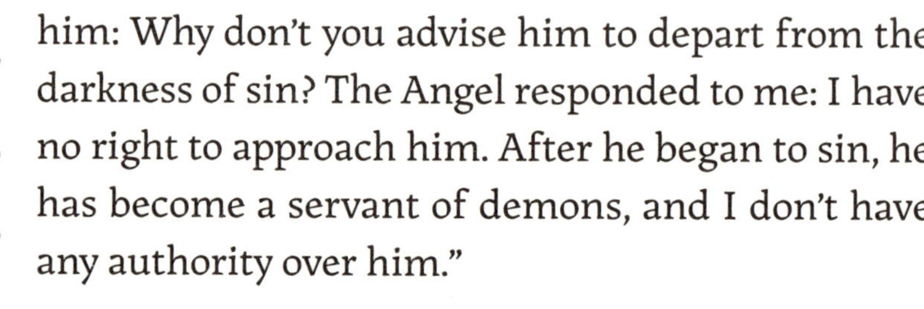

him: Why don't you advise him to depart from the darkness of sin? The Angel responded to me: I have no right to approach him. After he began to sin, he has become a servant of demons, and I don't have any authority over him."

At the end of the Exorcisms, the Priest breathes three times on the baptismal candidate and seals his forehead, chest and mouth saying: Drive out of *him / her* every evil and unclean spirit hiding and lurking in *his / her* heart.

The Renunciation of Satan

The renunciation of Satan and adherence to Christ is the final rite before Holy Baptism. The Priest, placing his hand on the head of the baptismal candidate, turns him towards the West and asks the following question three times: Do you renounce Satan? And all his works? And all his angels? And all his worship? And all his solemn rites?

And the Catechumen responds—or the Sponsor in the case of an infant—I renounce them!

By making this renunciation, the baptismal candidate confesses that he is being freed from demonic captivity, and avows to separate himself from such works and from the Devil's authority. Before making this renunciation, the candidate is turned towards the West, since this is the place of the Devil's kingdom, the outer darkness. This West-facing posture reminds the candidate of the darkness of his former life, and that by renouncing it, he is being transported to an illumined abode.

The completion of the rite of renunciation signifies that the candidate's former life, lived in separation from Christ, has ended. St. Gregory the Theologian says that Holy Baptism is an agreement with God to live a new and purified life. Every Orthodox Christian must carefully guard their own soul, so as not to trespass this confession!

What is the meaning of the candidate's professtion to be separated from the Devil's works, his angels, worship and solemn rites? The works of the Devil are every sinful deed. The angels of the Devil are the fallen angels, that is those who rebel against God. The worship of the Devil refers to fortune-telling, omens and superstitions, because all these are "iniquitous deeds of idolaters who have been snared in the Devil's trap." The solemn rites of the devil are, above all, masquerades and the madness of the theaters. St. Cyril of Jerusalem writes, "We ought not be interested in the madness of the theater, where you can see the indecent movements of the performers, with their mocking behavior and all sorts of other improprieties, and the frenzied dancing of effeminate men..." In our days, the solemn rites of the devil are naturally the spectacles presented on both television and the internet.

Concerning carnivals, we read in the martyrdom of St. Dasios (20 November): On New Year's Day, certain foolish people who called themselves

Christians, but who followed various pagan customs, donned costumes and marched around with great pomp in the manner and form of the Devil. They dressed in goat skins and disguised their faces, thereby abandoning the divine grace in which they were regenerated [baptized] for a return to their former evil ways. Though they had previously renounced the Devil and his solemn rites at Holy Baptism, they once again served him with their obscene and evil deeds!

After the Catechumen responds, I renounce him, three times, the Priest asks him again: Do you renounce Satan?

And the Catechumen (or the Sponsor) responds: I renounce him. When this has been repeated three times, the Priest says: Then blow and spit on him.

His breathing shows his heartfelt repudiation of the Devil. This is the reason that Priest exhorts him: Then blow on him. St. Symeon of Thessaloniki explains, "Thus he offers his heartfelt rejection of the Devil and shames the enemy. And the candidate for Holy Enlightenment does this three times, ensuring that he will in no way comply with demonic evil, and for the glorification of the Holy Trinity Who has conquered evil."

The life of the venerable Markianos mentions that the Saint crushed the Devil with the sign of the Cross and with a breath. Whenever the Saint prayed, a serpent (the symbol of the Devil) "sat up with his mouth open, angrily looking at the Saint, ready to attack him...making the sign of the Cross, the Saint breathed with his mouth and revealed the ancient enmity (between man and the Devil). Then the snake caught fire, glowing more brightly from the Saint's breath. Finally, it was totally engulfed in flames and was obliterated, just as happens to a reed that's burned.

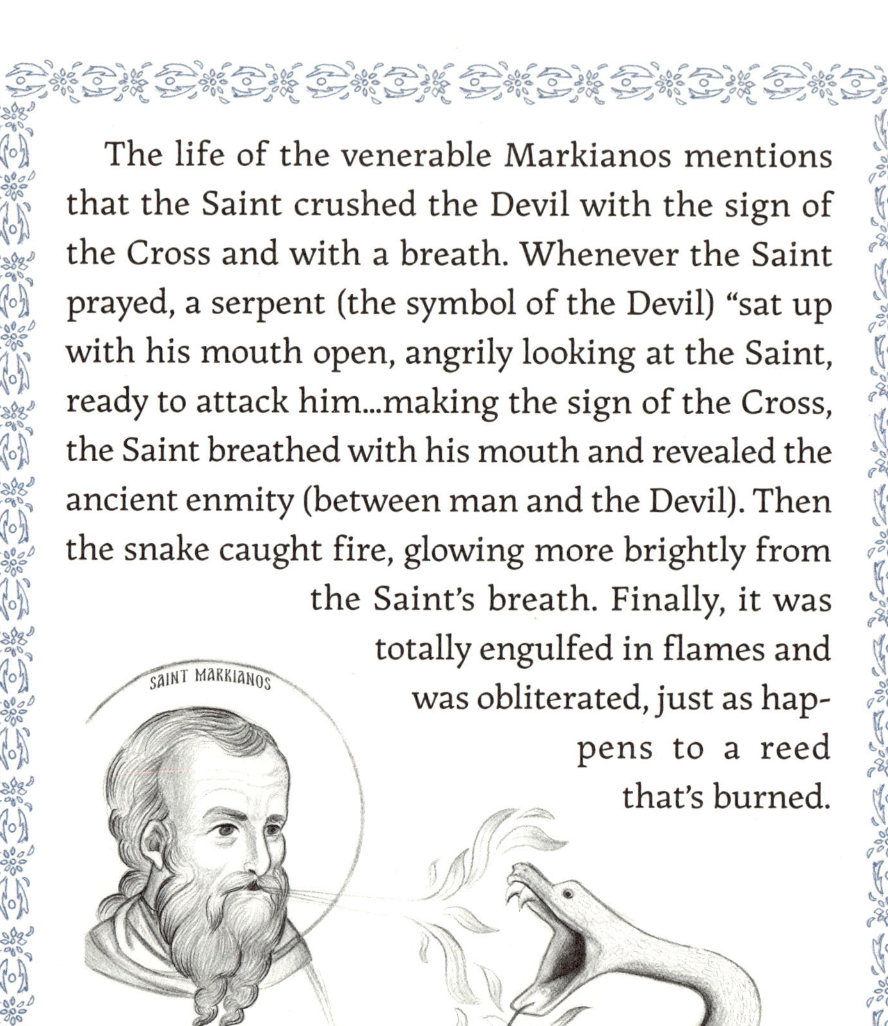

Adherence to Christ and the Confession of Faith

After the candidate for Illumination has separated himself from the Devil, the Priest turns him towards the East and asks three times: Do you unite yourself to Christ?

Each time the Priest asks, the Sponsor (or Catechumen) responds: I unite myself to Him, in other words, I promise Christ that after Holy Baptism, I will live in agreement with the divine commandments.

The candidate is now turned towards the East, because the East is a symbol of the Light. The East is the location of Paradise, which now opens its gates to receive the one to be illumined; Holy Baptism is the return of man to Paradise.

The Priest continues the rite by asking: Have you united yourself to Christ?

The candidate responds, I have united myself to Him.

And do you believe in Him?

I believe in Him as King and God.

After this final response, the candidate (or Sponsor) clearly states the entire confession of the Creed, the sacred Symbol of the Faith. This is done three times, first in order to confirm his confession, and the other times in honor of the Holy Trinity.

I BELIEVE IN ONE GOD, FATHER ALMIGHTY, CREATOR OF HEAVEN AND EARTH AND OF ALL THINGS VISIBLE AND INVISIBLE. AND IN ONE LORD JESUS CHRIST, THE ONLY-BEGOTTEN SON OF GOD, BEGOTTEN OF THE FATHER BEFORE ALL AGES. LIGHT OF LIGHT, TRUE GOD OF TRUE GOD, BEGOTTEN NOT CREATED, OF ONE ESSENCE WITH THE FATHER THROUGH WHOM ALL THINGS WERE MADE. WHO FOR US MEN AND FOR OUR SALVATION CAME DOWN FROM HEAVEN AND WAS INCARNATE OF THE HOLY SPIRIT AND THE VIRGIN MARY AND BECAME MAN. HE WAS CRUCIFIED FOR US UNDER PONTIUS PILATE. HE SUFFERED AND WAS BURIED...

The relationship between the confession of the Faith and the Mystery of Baptism is clearly shown in the story of the baptism of the **eunuch** courtier of Candace, queen of the Ethiopians. This event is described in the Acts of the Apostles. (Acts 8:36-39)

This courtier was returning to his home country by way of Jerusalem, where he had gone to wor-

ship. On the way he met the Apostle Philip, who, led by the Holy Spirit, proclaimed the joyful message about Christ and the salvation that He offers to believers. As they went on their way together, they arrived at a place with water, and the eunuch asked to be baptized. The Apostle Philip said: *If you believe with all your heart, you may.* And the eunuch responded, *I believe that Jesus Christ is the Son of God!* Then the two went down into the water and the Apostle baptized him. Immediately the Spirit of the Lord ascended from the water snatched Philip away, and the eunuch did not see him again. He continued on his journey filled with joy.

The final pre-baptismal priestly prayer—read just before the rite of Holy Baptism begins—summarizes in just a few words the divine gifts that the candidate for Enlightenment will receive: Count *him / her* worthy of the great grace of Your Holy Baptism. Put off *his / her* old self and renew *him / her* for eternal life and fill *him / her* with the power of Your Holy Spirit for union with Your Christ, that *he / she* may no longer be a child of the body, but a child of Your Kingdom.

With these words, the Priest beseeches the Lord to regenerate the candidate and to bestow upon him the grace of the Holy Spirit, so that he will no longer merely be a child of a fleshly birth, but a child of the Kingdom of God!

PART TWO
HOLY BAPTISM

The Mystery of Holy Baptism is the regeneration and rebirth of man by water and Spirit. St. John Chrysostom says that we are reborn at Holy Baptism. At our first birth, we are born from our mother's womb, while at Baptism we are reborn in the waters of the baptismal font. Like an embryo that takes shape within the watery womb, the faithful person is shaped and born in the baptismal waters. That is why the baptismal font is the womb of the Church: within it the faithful man is generated, and his emergence from it is his 'birth' day.

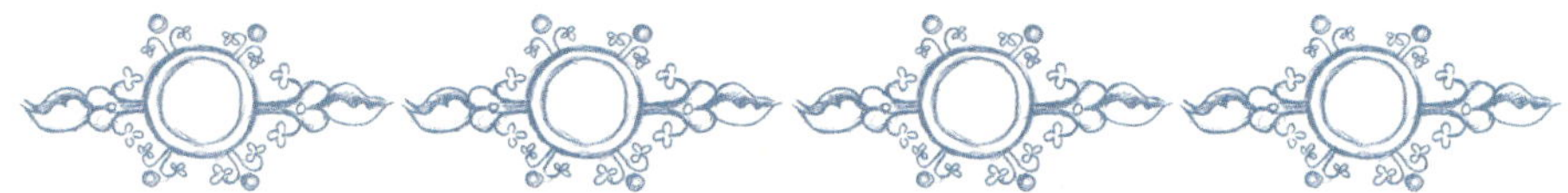

The Litany of Peace

Ever since apostolic times, Holy Baptism was celebrated during the Divine Liturgy. For this reason, the rite of Holy Baptism begins with the phrase, Blessed is the Kingdom of the Father... The Litany of Peace follows the doxology of the Kingdom of God—exactly as it happens in the Divine Liturgy. This is a series of petitions to which the people respond, Lord, have mercy. We pray for the peace of the whole world, for the sacred Temple, and all those who enter it with faith, piety and the fear of God. We pray for the Archbishop, the clergy and the people. We entreat the Lord for the sanctification of the waters, and for the salvation of the person who is approaching Holy Baptism.

The Priest commemorates the All-holy Mother of God at the end of the petitions. She is the cause of God becoming man, and her obedience to God's will allows us to become children and brethren of Christ.

Sanctification of the Water

In the next part of the Mystery, the water to be used for Holy Baptism is blessed by the Priest, and sanctified with the descent of the Holy Spirit.

The Priest proclaims with a loud voice: Great are You, O Lord, and wonderful are Your works; and no word will be adequate to sing the praise of Your wonders.

This exlamation is repeated three times. These words express the inexpressible: Praise of God's wonderful works, which are beyond human understanding and conception. What are God's marvelous works? They are His endless deeds that began with the creation of the world and His creation of man out of nothing. St. John Chrysostom says that we are "indebted to God for many deeds. He created us out of nothing. He sustains our life, and cares for us and the whole world. He oversees all of creation, whether visible or invisible, known or unknown." The most extraordinary of all divine gifts that we have received from Him is the Mystery of the Body of the Lord Jesus Christ. For our sake, God did not even spare His only begotten Son—and so it is right to hymn, bless and give lasting thanks to Him!"

In the prayer of the sanctification of the waters, we hear that, together with mankind, all of creation participates in the doxology of the Creator! ...The sun sings Your praises, the moon glorifies You, the stars entreat You...Angelic Powers minister to You, the choirs of Archangels worship You...

St. John Chrysostom interprets the 19th Psalm, *The heavens declare the glory of God*, "How does the heaven declare it? It speaks even when it is silent!...That is, when you behold its beauty, grandeur, position, its stability over the passage of time, and its brilliance, you glorify and praise the Creator crying out: Glory to You, O God! What a great foundation You established! The heavens reply by using the language of their own glory."

The sun, moon, stars, Angels and Archangels comprise a "common assembly of a single choir from the entire creation," to which man himself is invited.

The prayer of sanctification continues, For You, God uncircumscribed, without beginning and ineffable, came upon earth, taking the form of a slave, being found in the likeness of mortals...For You, our God, were seen on earth and lived among mankind... Christ is truly the Son of God who became the Son of man to make mankind children of God. Man lived in the darkness of sin, so God dispersed the darkness with the light of His presence. Humanity was ill, so the most capable physician prepared medicines for our salvation. As an antidote, He gave us Holy Baptism, which imparted strength to our soul and gave us the possibility of becoming a new creation.

You also sanctified the streams of the Jordan by sending upon them Your All-holy Spirit from Heaven... Christ was not baptized in the Jordan River on account of any personal need, but because Baptism needed His power. St. John Chrysostom explains, "The Lord of the Angels descended into the riverbed of the Jordan and then sanctified the nature of the waters, healing the entire world."

At this moment, the Priest exclaims: Therefore, O King, Lover of mankind, be present now too, through the visitation of Your Holy Spirit, and sanctify this water. While repeating this three times, the Priest makes the sign of the Cross in the water with his hand. Thus the water of

the baptismal font is blessed by the Celebrant, and it is sanctified with the descent of the Holy Spirit.

Shortly after this, the Priest breathes on the water crosswise, and seals the waters three times again while exclaiming: Let all adverse powers be crushed beneath the sign of the image of Your Cross. The Celebrant entreats God to crush the demonic powers by making the sign of the Cross. He makes this entreaty because the power of the precious Cross and the Name of our Lord Jesus Christ is a fire which utterly devours the Devil. The precious Cross is the symbol of Christ's victory. For this reason, whether we are to be regenerated by Holy Baptism, or we are to be fed with Holy Communion, or whatever else we might do, this symbol of our salvation and liberation is always present.

Once they led four demoniacs to blessed John Astrino for Divine Services. These demon-possessed men often spoke by the power of the Devil. When John heard them, he asked them many things including:

Why do you fear Christians?

There are three fundamental reasons: One you wear around your neck, another is where you are washed in the Church, and yet another you eat at.

They meant the precious Cross, Holy Baptism, and Holy Communion.

The pious John asked another question:

What religion do you prefer amongst all those on the earth?

We love all those that do not have those three things we mentioned and do not confess God or Son of God, the son of Mary. The Devil's demons revealed all this and more in front of many who saw and heard what they said.

After the Celebrant supplicates the all-holy Name of the Lord, he seals the water with the sign of the life-creating Cross. Then he asks the Lord to grant the water power to liberate from the bonds of sin, and to make the baptismal font into a fountain of incorrupt life. But do You, Master of all things, declare this water to be water of redemption, water of sanctification, cleansing of flesh and spirit, untying of bonds, forgiveness of offenses, enlightenment of soul, washing of rebirth, renewal of spirit, gift of adoption, garment of incorruption, and source of life. For it was You, Lord, who said,

'Wash and be made clean, and put away evils from your souls.' Everyone who is baptized receives the forgiveness of Original Sin. Baptism even forgives the sins of those who crucified Christ!

In the Acts of the Apostles (2:37-38), we read what happened on Pentecost when the Apostle Peter spoke to those whose iniquitous hands crucified the Lord: *Now when the people heard this, they were cut to the heart and asked Peter and the rest of the apostles, "Brethren, what shall we do?" Peter said to them, "Repent, and be baptized, every one of you, in the Name of Jesus Christ, for the forgiveness of sins, and you will receive the gift of the Holy Spirit."*

The Priest continues, It is You who have given us the grace of rebirth from on high through water and Spirit. And this is exactly what happens at Holy Baptism—the person baptized is born of God in the Church. The Mystery of Holy Baptism is the birth of a new person, and the beginning of his life in Christ. The image of God is restored at the Mystery—the image which fell and was shattered because of evil. Manifest Yourself, Lord, in this water, and grant that the one being baptized in it may be transformed for the putting off of the old self that is corrupted by the desires of deception, and may put on the new self that is renewed after the image of the One who created *him / her*.

The Priest concludes, For to You belong glory, might, honor and worship, together with Your Father Who is without beginning, and Your all-holy, good, and life-giving Spirit, now and for ever, and to the ages of ages, having now completed the prayer of the sanctification of the waters.

Sanctification of the Oil

After the water has been sanctified, the Priest blesses the oil that will be used for the Baptism. He begins by blowing on the container of oil three times, and then seals it with the sign of the Cross. Next, he reads the prayer for the sanctification of the oil, and anoints the candidate for Holy Enlightenment.

Addressing the candidates, St. John Chrysostom says, "After the renunciation of the Devil, after the adherence to Christ, after you have become the Lord's and have no concourse with the Devil, then the Priest is directed to immediately seal you with oil in the sign of the Cross on your forehead. The Priest signs your face to crush every madness of the Devil, since the Devil would not dare to cast his gaze on someone who has been signed with the Cross. Rather, seeing the rays of light transmitted from it, he flees unsatisfied."

The prayer for the sanctification of the oil begins with a remembrance of the Flood, and the olive-branch carrying dove that announced to Noah and to his household the abatement of the flood waters: Master, Lord God of our fathers, Who sent out a dove to those in Noah's ark, with a branch of olive in its beak as a sign of reconciliation and salvation from the Flood, and through these things prefigured the Mystery of Grace...do You Yourself bless this olive oil also by the power, operation and descent of Your Holy Spirit.

What does this mean? When the storm ended, Noah released a dove from the ark in order to ascertain the conditions outside. He wanted to know what his family, and the animals, would encounter if they left the ark. Not long after being released, the dove returned carrying a olive branch. This was a sign that the waters had sufficiently receded, and that Noah and his family could safely leave the ark. The flood waters prefigured the water of Holy Baptism—the dove signified the Holy Spirit, and the olive branch carried in the dove's beak was a sign of divine mercy and God's infinite goodness. That's why the anointing with olive oil teaches us that baptismal reconciliation is a divine gift that is an expression of God's mercy.

As the Priest continues, holding the container of holy oil in his hand, he pours it into the baptismal font with the sign of the Cross, while at the same time chanting Alleluia. After this, he exclaims: Blessed is God, Who enlightens and sanctifies everyone who comes into the world, now and for ever, and to the ages of ages.

The God-bearing Fathers call the Mystery of Holy Baptism "Enlightenment," because when a person is baptized he is enlightened and sanctified. Before Holy Baptism, mankind lived in the darkness, with this Mystery he enters into the world of light.

St. Dionysios the Areopagite explains: It is "common knowledge that in all the Mysteries the transmission of divine light is imparted to the initiates." However, Holy Baptism is the first "that imparts divine vision, and by exposure to the origin of light, guides them to the experience of all the other sacred Mysteries." After a person becomes a son of light, he maintains the bright garment of his soul by living a God-pleasing life, and in this way endures as a neophyte for his whole life. In other words, he perpetually lives in the paradisiacal brillance into which God has invested him at Holy Baptism!

The moment has arrived when the baptismal candidate will be anointed with holy oil. The Priest, using the three fingers of his right hand, takes some of the holy oil and makes the sign of the Cross on the baptismal candidate's forehead, chest, back, hands and feet. The servant of God, *N.*, is anointed with the oil of gladness, in the Name of the Father, and of the Son, and of the Holy Spirit. Amen.

As we said previously, at the Mystery of Holy Baptism, man enters into the world of light and becomes a friend of the common Master of all. That is why this anointing oil is called the oil of gladness—it denotes that the Church welcomes this event with great joy.

Now the Celebrant seals the chest exclaiming: For healing of soul and body.

And the ears saying: For the hearing of faith.

And the feet: For your feet to walk.

And the hands: Your hands made me and fashioned me.

After these exclamations, the Sponsor anoints the whole body of the baptismal candidate, which is a symbol of recreation, but also of the entrance of the person into the arena of spiritual struggle.

In ancient times, athletes—primarily wrestlers—were anointed with oil before their match so that their opponents would be unable to easily take hold of them. The battle with, and resistance against, the Devil begins from this moment. Thus, the Priest stands before an athlete, anoints him with oil and leads him into the spiritual arena.

The baptismal candidate is given the life-creating Cross as a weapon for his spiritual struggles. By the power of the Cross, the new Christian will be able to contend with the spiritual struggles of life, and to prevail over his great enemies—the passions and the demons.

Baptism

The servant of God *N.* is baptized, in the Name of the Father. Amen. And of the Son. Amen. And of the Holy Spirit. Amen.

After the Sponsor anoints the candidate's entire body with olive oil, the Priest plunges him into the water of the baptismal font three times, while facing eastward. In the Name of the Father. Amen. And of the Son. Amen. And of the Holy Spirit. Amen.

This triple immersion and invocation of the Holy Trinity is the decisive moment of the celebration of the Mystery. With the triple immersion into the baptismal font and emersion from it, the essential meaning of the Mystery is clearly shown: With Holy Baptism, the human person dies together with Christ, is buried and rises again with Him. In Holy Baptism, everything happens at the same time: death and the entombment of the old man, and resurrection of the new per-

THE THREE IMMERSIONS OF THE CHILD...

son. This wondrous transformation, in which the old man is buried and emerges completely regenerated, is effortless for the all-powerful Creator of Heaven and Earth!

We read the following account in the life of St. Drosida, the daughter of the emperor Trajan: During the reign of her father Trajan, about the year 99AD, any person who confessed Christ suffered severe persecution. This impious king made sure to scatter the remains of the holy martyrs in unclean and disgraceful places.

Nevertheless, some Christians secretly took the relics from such places and buried them. In order to learn who was stealing the bodies—with the intention of punishing these relic-thieves—the emperor ordered some soldiers to safeguard the remains of the martyred Christians.

To his great shock, the guards arrested five monks and his daughter Drosida! The emperor ordered the monks be put to death, while he ordered that his daughter be put under guard in a secure location, with the hope that she might repent.

A little later, Trajan, full of fury for the Christians, ordered two enormous ovens be stoked on each side of the city with the following inscription: "Men of Galilee, you who worship the Crucified

One, save yourselves from suffering, and us from the effort, and cast yourselves into whichever oven you wish."

Upon hearing this order, Drosida raised her eyes to heaven and said: "Master and Lord, Jesus Christ, Son of God, if it is Your holy will to save and redeem me from the wicked religion of my father Trajan and ascend to heaven, cause these guards to sleep so that I may escape unnoticed."

Saying these words, she took off her royal robes and calmly left the palace, without anyone noticing. But just as she was about to cast herself into one of the ovens, she thought to herself: How will I go to Heaven unclean and without a wedding garment, and without having first received Holy Baptism? Nevertheless my Lord, who knows that I have surrendered my royal inheritance, baptize me by the Holy Spirit!

And just as she had said these words, she took the myrrh which she had kept in her room, and anointed her body with it and then baptized herself in a nearby lake, saying: The servant of God Drosida is baptized in the name of the Father and of the Son and of the Holy Spirit.

From that moment and for the next seven days, she hid herself, while an Angel of the Lord brought food to her every day. She told these things to some Christians who happened to discover her location. On the eighth day, while they were in prayer, seeking divine guidance about what they should do, her soul departed for the Lord."

What is the meaning of the triple immersion of the baptismal candidate? St. Cyril of Jerusalem says that this triple immersion, "symbolizes the three-day entombment of Christ. Just as our Savior remained buried in the heart of the earth for three days and three nights, so do you." So, just like a dead body is buried and completely covered with earth, the baptis-

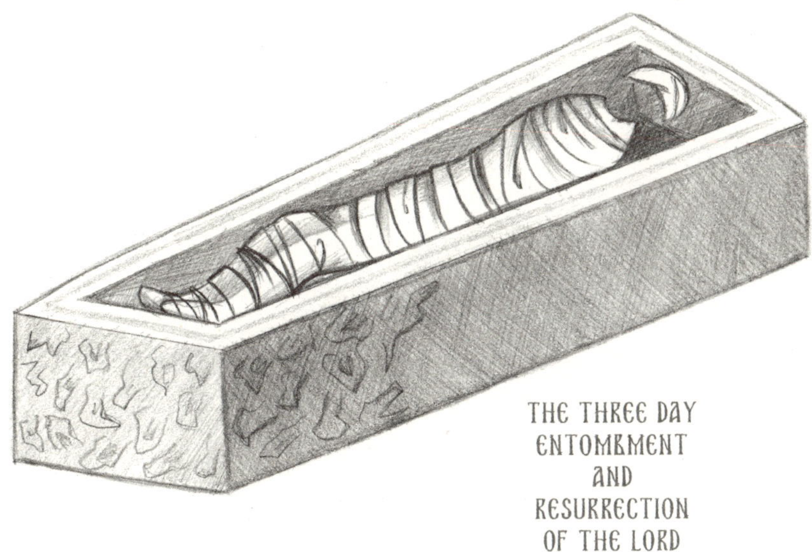

THE THREE DAY ENTOMBMENT AND RESURRECTION OF THE LORD

mal candidate's body is also completely covered—not merely one part of the body—with water.

GO AND MAKE DISCIPLES OF ALL NATIONS, BAPTIZING THEM IN THE NAME OF THE FATHER AND OF THE SON AND OF THE HOLY SPIRIT,

St. John Chrysostom explains that we are immersed three times "in order to teach that everything, every divine gift, given in Holy Baptism, is the power and operation of the Father, and the Son, and the Holy Spirit." The Priest is merely a servant of the grace of the Holy Trinity. "The one who officiates is the Father, and the Son and the Holy Spirit, the indivisible Trinity. Faith in the Holy Trinity grants the remission of sins, while our confession grants us sonship."

After a person's triple emersion from the baptismal waters, he is called *newly illumined*. Subsequently, the person—if it is an infant—is returned to his Sponsor, who then wraps the child in a white sheet.

The choir sings the 31st Psalm: *Blessed is the man*...etc.

This Psalm of David speaks of repentance, and beautifully expresses the joy of a sinful person who has returned to the Lord. It is precisely for this reason that this Psalm has been linked to the Mystery of Holy Baptism since ancient times.

Be glad in the Lord and rejoice, you righteous; And shout for joy, all you upright in heart! concludes the Psalmist. Man's return to the heavenly Father, who officiates at Holy Baptism, is a cause of joy! Heaven and earth delight together! At the moment a human person is regenerated, holy Angels are present and surround the Triune God in silence.

At Holy Baptism, Christ makes our soul—which was darkened by sin—beautiful by His love. He transforms our ugliness and exchanges it with His own beauty, and makes us participants of His own goodness. In the sacred baptismal font, Christ buries the deformity of the old man, and then gives us a share in His own magnificence, making us something new and bright.

St. Cyril of Jerusalem writes, "The moment when you enter the Church like stars, with your bodies bright and your souls shining, the Angels will chant: *Blessed are those whose iniquities are forgiven.*" (Ps. 31:1)

On the 4th of November, the Church honors St. Porphyrios the Mime. Porphyrios was raised in Ephesus and, from an early age, studied the art of acting.

One day, at the behest of Count Alexander, a large audience gathered in the theater in order to watch a performance. The purpose of this performance was to mock the Holy Mysteries of the Church. The actors dressed as bishops, priests, deacons and chanters.

Porphyrios, who had a leading role, had been chosen to portray a person who was going to be baptized by the other actors. An actress, who was

playing the role of Bishop, put him in the water to baptize him in the Name of the Holy Trinity. Afterwards, he got out of the baptismal font and dressed in white clothing as is customary for a newly baptized person. At this point, they planned to begin to mock Christ and the Church.

However, something unexpected happened. The Holy Spirit overshadowed Porphyrios, and instead of mocking the Christian faith, he began to doxologize God, as if he were truly a Christian! At the very moment that all of this was happening, the entire city was violently shaken by an earthquake and radiant angels appeared in the theater. They carried lit candles and preceded Porphyrios while chanting and praising God. Afterwards, they taught him how to pray as an Orthodox Christian.

The audience was dumbfounded and were saying amongst themselves, "If Porphyrios' sham baptism has this sort of power, then how much more power will God grant to those who are truly baptized!?" At this, a great multitude from the crowd drew near to Porphyrios and begged him to baptize them!

The Saint then turned towards the East and prayed for the people, as the Angels had instructed him. Immediately, a shining cloud descended from heaven overshadowing the theater, and it began to rain on the people and enlightened those who believed in Christ. In this way, many from the audience were baptized in the Name of the Holy Trinity. Then, the people left the theater following the holy Angels towards the Church.

When they entered the Church, it was brightly illuminated by the Angels' brilliance. The newly illumined then knelt down and prayed for a long time. After they had finished praying and stood up, the Angels had vanished, leaving their souls filled with unspeakable joy!

ΩΝ
SAINT CHRI STINA

The Mystery of Sacred Chrismation

Immediately after the Baptism, the Priest silently says the prayer of the Holy Myrrh, Do You then, Master, compassionate, universal King, grant *him/her* also the Seal of the gift of Your of all-powerful Holy Spirit, Who is worthy of all honor and worship, and then, after the prayer is completed, he anoints the newly baptized with the Holy Myrrh by making the sign of the Cross on the forehead, eyes, nose, mouth, ears, chest, hands and feet, while repeating the words: The Seal of the gift of the Holy Spirit. Amen.

The following miracle is recorded in the life of the holy great martyr Christina (24th July): When her father Urban saw how he was unable to convert his daughter Christina to an idol worshipper, he ordered his servants to tie a huge stone around the Saint's neck, and to throw her into the sea. However,

the Lord did not leave his servant unprotected, but immediately sent Angels to untie it, and it sank to the bottom of the sea. The servants were astonished to see the Saint joyfully walking upon the waves, and glorifying God.

"My Lord, thank You for the love which You have shown me, Your humble servant. I beg You, make me worthy to receive Holy Baptism in these waters, so that all my sins might be forgiven!"

Then she heard a voice from the heavens saying: "Christina, I have heard your request."

At that very moment a bright cloud suddenly appeared and upon it was the Lord Jesus Christ. He was dressed in royal purple and there was a shining crown upon His head. All around Him were Angels chanting and censing Him with fragrant incense. When Christina saw the Lord, she fell to her knees and worshipped Him. He raised her up and said to her:

"Christina, I am Jesus Christ, and I illumine everyone who calls upon me. I heard your prayer, and I came to redeem you from the deception of the idols, just as you asked me to do."

Then He descended into the sea saying: "Christina, I baptize you in the Name of my Father, and in the name of His Son, and in the Holy Spirit."

Afterwards, He returned to where the Archangel Michael stood, for he had accompanied the Lord.

"Illumine her with My seal and lead her to the shore." The saint received the Mystery of Holy Chrism from the Archangel and then was miraculously translated to the city, where she was found next to her father's house! And there she stood in prayer until the morning.

St. Mark the Evangelist wrote that when Christ was baptized in the Jordan River by St. John the Forerunner, *Immediately coming up from the water, he saw the heavens torn open and the Spirit descending on Him like a dove. A voice came out of the heavens, 'You are My beloved Son. In You I am well pleased.'*

Whereas the Baptism of Jesus Christ by the honorable Forerunner constitutes the beginning of the Mystery of Holy Baptism, the descent of the All-holy Spirit upon the Lord constitutes the beginning of the mystery of Holy Chrism. For this reason, immediately after Holy Baptism, the Mystery of Holy Chrism is officiated.

St. John Chrysostom says that the All-holy Spirit came to the Lord at His baptism "in order to reveal the identity of the Son of God to those present and to St. John. And not only for this reason, but also to teach us that when we are baptized, the Holy Spirit comes to us."

In the Gerontikon we read the following story:

One day a certain brother happened to be attacked by a great temptation which led him to renounce God, his Baptism, and his monastic vows. Immediately he saw something like a dove come out of his mouth and fly into the heavens.

A little later, he came to his senses and repented. He departed for the desert to be near a certain great elder, and told him about his struggle. The elder said to him: "Stay with me in my cave for three weeks, fast, and I will entreat God on your behalf." And this is what happened—the elder prayed fervently to God and begged Him to accept the brother's repentance. And God heard him.

Just as the first week was completed, the elder asked the brother, "Did you see anything?" And the

brother answered, "I saw a dove hovering high in the sky, opposite me." The elder encouraged him to continue the struggle saying, "Watch yourself carefully, and persist in your entreaty to God!"

When the second week was completed, the elder again asked the brother, "Did you see anything?" And he told him, "I saw that dove hover, but it was lower and nearer to my head." The elder insisted that he zealously continue his regimen of prayer and fasting. At the end of the third week, the elder visited the brother and asked him, "Did you see anything?" The brother said, "I saw that dove come and hover right on my head, and I opened my hands for him, and then immediately he flew right into my mouth."

The elder thanked God and said to the brother, "God has received your repentance. Hereafter, watch over yourself carefully!"

That brother, desiring to be near the elder, remained in the cave until the end of his life!

The descent of the Comforter upon the anointed shows that he is a son of God by grace. The gift of the Holy Spirit, which a person receives when he is anointed, is the confirmation of God in him, that he will live according to His will and will thus be shown to be His beloved son.

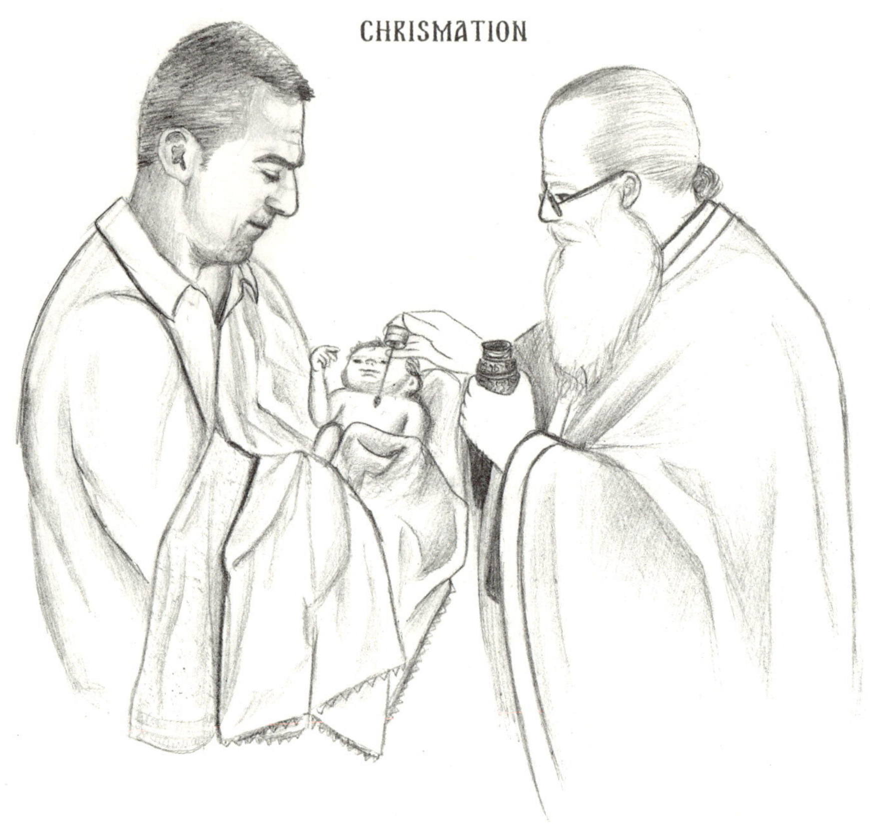

Holy Chrism is the restoration of man to his former glory. When man was created, God breathed life into him, creating him after His own image. This Seal, which Adam and Eve shattered by disobedience, is restored at the Mystery of Chrismation. Those who are sealed are recognized by Christ and the holy Angels because they have been distinguished as icons of God.

With the Seal of the gift of the Holy Spirit, we become part of the flock of the Good Shepherd, Jesus Christ. The Devil—the noetic wolf— does not dare oppose the Archpastor's sheep, because they have been branded with the Seal of the

Holy Spirit. These marked sheep are well protected, while the unmarked are easily snatched.

Why does the Celebrant of the Mystery seal the newly illumined on all the members of the body? St. Cyril of Jerusalem explains that, "First, you are anointed on the forehead in order to liberate you from shame which the transgressor Adam carried with him everywhere...Then you were anointed on the ears so that you might acquire ears like those described by the Lord in the Gospel: *Anyone who has ears for listening should listen!* After the ears, your nostrils were anointed so that smelling the spiritual Myrrh, you will say: *Indeed, we are a sweet fragrance of Christ to God, both in those who are being saved and in those who are perishing.* Finally, you were anointed on the chest, *so that having put on the breastplate of righteousness* (Eph. 6:14), *you may be able to resist the Devil's tactics* (Eph. 6:11).

In other words, the baptized person receives the Seal of the Holy Spirit by dedicating himself completely—senses, manner of life and heart—to Christ. In this way, the grace of the Holy Spirit sanctifies the entire person. Christ wants the person whom He has loved with the Mystery of Holy Baptism to have Himself impressed upon him, so that in act and in thought, he thinks of Christ alone, and nothing else.

THE RETURN OF THE PRODIGAL SON

The Vesting of the Newly Illumined

In the early Church, before the practice of infant baptism became prevalent, the vesting of the newly illumined took place immediately after Baptism and before Chrismation. Today, the Celebrant of the Mystery typically vests the newly illumined after the anointment of the Holy Chrism. He prays, The servant of God *N.* is clothed with a garment of righteousness, in the Name of the Father, and of the Son, and of the Holy Spirit. Amen. And the chanters sing: Grant me a tunic of light, O most merciful, Christ our God, Who wrap Yourself in light as in a garment.

In the parable of the prodigal son, we read that the Father was lovingly waiting for His son to return to His house. When he finally did return, He embraced His son and kissed him affectionately. And as soon as the prodigal son confessed that he had sinned against his Father's love and was unworthy to be called His son, the Father said to His servants: *Bring out the*

first robe and put it on him! Put a ring on his hand and shoes on his feet! Bring the fattened calf, kill it, and let us eat and celebrate. (Luke 15:22-23)

The God-bearing Fathers believe that these loving words of the prodigal son's father, an icon of God the Father, characterize the grace of the Holy Mysteries, by which a person enters into the paternal House, the Church—Holy Baptism, Divine Chrismation and Holy Communion. At Holy Baptism, a person is regenerated and vested in the garment of mankind's former glory *(...and put it on him...)*. Then, at Holy Chrismation, he receives the ring, that is, the Seal of the gift of the Holy Spirit (*...Put a ring on his hand...*). And finally, at Holy Communion, he participates in the Lord's Table (*...let us eat and celebrate...*)

The garment of the newly illumined person is white. It's white color expresses the joyful proclamation of the Church at the return of a formerly lost child of God.

We learn something about white baptismal garments in life of the venerable ascetic Anthousa and the martyrdom of St. Leontios.

The venerable ascetic Anthousa, whose memory is celebrated on August 22, was the daughter of wealthy idolaters. Having secretly come to faith in Christ, she longed to be baptized. She desired to meet Bishop Athanasios who preached about the faith in Tarsus of Cilicia.

One day, she convinced her mother to allow her to go into the city on the pretext of visiting her nurse. While traveling there with two servants, something wondrous happened. Bishop Athanasios was transported by two holy angels and appeared on the very road Anthousa was traveling. When St. Anthousa learned that the person standing before her was Bishop Athanasios—the person she was secretly planning to meet—she fell at his feet and begged him to baptize her. Since there was no water nearby, St. Athanasios began to pray, and at once a gushing spring emerged out of the earth. Here, the Saint received Holy Baptism, together with her two servants. Within the water stood two angels dressed as soldiers, who dressed the Saint in white garments. Following her Baptism, Anthousa gave St. Athanasios the precious gold-woven garments she was wearing, so that he might give them to the

THE TRANSFIGURATION

poor. Some time later, Anthousa was tonsured a nun. She lived for twenty years in the desert, after which she departed this life in peace.

In the martyrdom of St. Leontios we read the following:

Leontios was a general in the Roman army who openly lived the Christian life—he also taught others about Christ. When Adrianos, the Phoenician governor, learned about his general's activities, he sent a tribune of soldiers, led by a certain Ipatos and Theodoulos, to convince him to stop. On their way to see Leontios, Ipatos was stricken, but miraculously healed after seeing an Angelic vision and invoking the true God three times. When they found Leontios, the two soldiers fell at his feet, and begged to be united to Christ. Upon hearing their request, St. Leontios prayed to God for them. Immediately, a rain cloud descended from heaven and provided the water necessary for the soldiers' Baptism. After their Illumination, Leontios dressed them in white garments. Not long after this, they all received the unfading crown of martyrdom. The Church celebrates the memory of Ipatos, Theodoulos and Leontios on June 18.

The bright white garments, with which a newly illumined Christian are vested, symbolize the Lord's clothing. According to Holy Scripture, at His Transfiguration, His garments *became as white as the light.* (Mt 17:2) It is also an icon of the resurrection, and a sign of the promise of eternal life.

Taking this into account, St. John Chrysostom admonishes the newly illumined Christians to keep their baptismal garments clean. "Now that you have been vested in Christ, and have received the inspiration of the Holy Spirit, take care to keep your baptismal garments gleaming, without spot or wrinkle—speak carefully, do not listen to vanities, shun evil suggestive thoughts (logismoi), and close your eyes to those things which ought not be seen."

In the **Spiritual Meadow**, we find a story about a certain newly illumined Christian. "After Holy Baptism the eyes of his soul were opened and he saw the angelic powers and everything that was secretly celebrated by them...this neophyte saw these visions when he donned the new white clothing filled with light. When however, he removed them, he no longer saw any more visions.

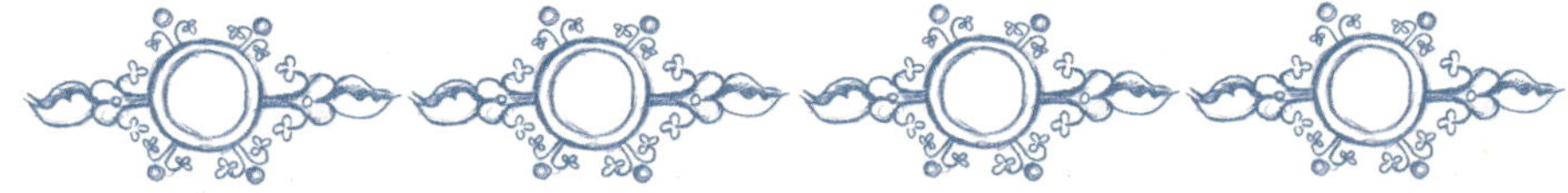

The Divine Liturgy and Holy Baptism

The Mystery of Holy Baptism is usually closely connected with Holy Communion. Following baptismal regeneration and Holy Christmation, the newly illumined is immediately invited to participate in the Lord's Table.

St. John the Evangelist stresses the close link between Holy Baptism and Holy Communion, citing two events from the final days of our Lord's earthly life.

The first event happened in the evening at the Mystical Supper. Before the Lord gave the disciples His Body and immaculate Blood, He washed their feet. This act was a symbol of Holy Baptism. For a person to participate in the Mystical Supper, it presupposes the "cleansing" of Holy Baptism.

The second incident happened when the Lord's side was pierced while hanging on the Cross. At that moment, Blood and water flowed out of His side—the water symbolizes Holy

Baptism, and the Blood, Holy Communion. Therefore, we can say that the Holy Mysteries of the Church pour forth from the Lord's Body!

During apostolic times, Holy Baptism was celebrated during the Divine Liturgy. The newly illumined were vested in white, holding lit candles and chanted from the Psalms. They followed the Bishop and Presbyters and took their place on the solea in front of the Sanctuary. From there, they participated in the Divine Liturgy and received Holy Communion.

Today, Baptism is typically celebrated outside the service of the Divine Liturgy, though certain ancient elements remain.

For example, there is an Epistle and Gospel reading like in the Divine Liturgy. The ancient entrance of the newly illumined into the Church has also been retained. Shortly after the newly illumined has been baptized and anointed, he and his Sponsor follow the Priest in a procession around the baptismal font. During this procession, the Priest censes the font while the chanters joyfully sing the following hymn: All those who have been baptized into Christ have put on Christ. Alleluia.

In the Leimonarion, we find the story of a certain 17-year-old who was baptized by St. John the Merciful on Pascha. "When I was baptized," the neophyte explains, "I came out of the water, and then St. John anointed me. After this happened, I saw some shadowy person come out of my body, and someone else, about my age—an Angel of the Lord—white as the sun, armed like a soldier, who came and stood by my right hand and guarded me. When we began to chant, All those who have been baptized, suddenly many Angels entered the Church—they were friends of my guardian Angel! Then these angels processed in front of us as we made our way from the baptistry to the Church. They continued their march until they entered the Sanctuary and encircled the Holy Table. They remained there concelebrating the Divine Liturgy with the priests until the end of the service.

1. The Epistle Reading

The first **pericope** is taken from the Epistle of St. Paul to the Romans. It summarizes the Church's teaching about the Mystery of Holy Baptism.

Brethren, do you not know that all of us who were baptized into Christ were baptized into his death... At Holy Baptism, the baptismal candidate imitates the crucifixion and entombment of Christ, and is then resurrected into the new life in Christ.

"The strange thing is," writes St. Cyril of Jerusalem, "we did not really die, nor were we really buried, or crucified or resurrected. Indeed, this all happened symbolically, though our salvation is real! Christ truly died, was buried, and rose again...all of these He has freely made ours, that by sharing His sufferings in a symbolic way, we may really and truly gain salvation."

It means that we recognize this, that our old humanity was crucified with Him, so that body of sin might be done away with... At Holy Baptism, we are crucified and buried together with Christ. However, whereas Christ experienced bodily death and entombment, we experience the death and entombment of our sins. The new life, which begins at Holy Baptism, becomes a living reality when a person endures as though dead to sin. He lives his spiritual calling when he shuns hedonistic pleasures, is not consumed by the love of money, refuses to slander his fellow man, and always speaks the truth. Indeed, the baptized Christian is called to spurn the delights of the world, and seek after the things of heaven.

2. The Gospel Reading

After the Epistle, the Priest reads from the Holy Gospel. The newly illumined and his Sponsor listen to the reading while standing before the **Beautiful Gate**.

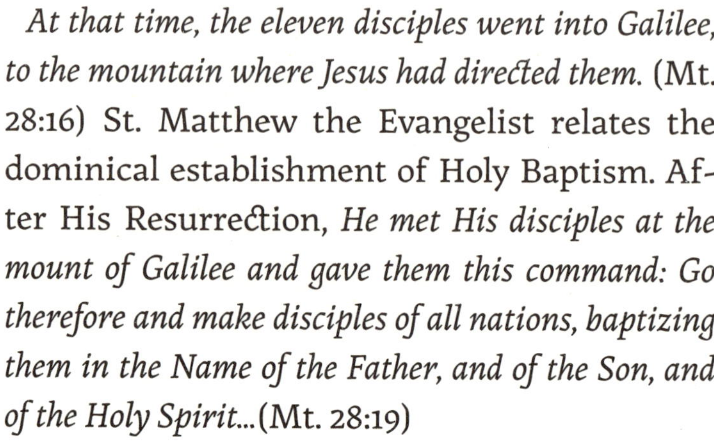

At that time, the eleven disciples went into Galilee, to the mountain where Jesus had directed them. (Mt. 28:16) St. Matthew the Evangelist relates the dominical establishment of Holy Baptism. After His Resurrection, *He met His disciples at the mount of Galilee and gave them this command: Go therefore and make disciples of all nations, baptizing them in the Name of the Father, and of the Son, and of the Holy Spirit...*(Mt. 28:19)

The Lord did not merely order His disciples to baptize. He also taught them how to baptize—in the name of the Holy Trinity. Why? Because spiritual advancement requires that correct faith be joined to correct practice.

When the Lord said, *teaching them to observe all the things that I have commanded you* (Mt. 28:20), He meant that a true follower "is one who comes to the Lord for the purpose of following Him, that is, to hear His words, to believe in Him and obey Him as Master, King, Physician, and Teacher of truth, in the hope of gaining eternal life. Further, he must persevere in these dispositions..." Because as St. Basil writes, "we are under the strictest obligation...to free ourselves from the dominion of the Devil who leads a slave of sin into evils, even against his will."

St. John Chrysostom explains that the phrase, *Go therefore and make disciples of all nations* (Mt. 28:19), refers to the dogmas of the Church, *whereas teaching them to observe all the things that I have commanded you* (Mt. 28:20) refers to the Lord's commandments. Therefore, after learning the faith we are baptized—then begins the struggle for the acquisition of the virtues.

Holy Communion

If the Mystery of Baptism occurs during the Divine Liturgy, then the newly illumined Christian receives the Body and Blood of Christ during its celebration. St. Nikodemos of the Holy Mountain encourages that the Divine Liturgy be celebrated immediately following Holy Baptism, "so that the a person who has been baptized might commune." He explains that "it is natural for a newly born infant to drink milk. Likewise, as soon as a person is spiritually reborn at the Mystery of Holy Baptism, he is ready, by divine grace, to receive the spiritual food of Holy Communion."

This spiritual food is Christ Himself. He feeds those whom He has spiritually reborn—at Baptism—with His own Body. In this way, Christ becomes our Father, for we are baptized into His Name, as well as our Mother, because He immediately feeds us following our spiritual birth.

HOLY COMMUNION

The newly illumined, now a member of the Church, is able to commune of the Body and Blood of Christ. Thus, the fullness of divine love for mankind is offered in these three Mysteries: Holy Baptism, Divine Chrismation, and Holy Communion.

We read the following in the lives of the holy brother martyrs Evstathios, Thespesios, and Anatolios (303AD). Their father, Philotheos, was a fabric merchant. One day, he went on a journey with his business partner Patrophilos, and two of his children. On their journey, they met St. Loukianos, a certain Presbyter from **Antioch** and future martyr of the Church. Loukianos asked them: "Which God do you worship?" They responded, "the Sun." In response to this, the Saint taught them about the true God, Creator of the heavens and the earth. He preached to them about Jesus Christ and the Mystery of His incarnation, and urged them to have faith in Him and to be baptized, so that they might enter the Kingdom of Heaven. After teaching them, they arrived at the Sangarius river where the whole company entreated the Saint to baptize them. Standing on the river's edge, the Saint told them to prepare white garments. After this, the Saint blessed oil in his hands and anointed them with it, and then baptized them in the name of the Father, and the Son, and the Holy Spirit, to which they replied Amen. After coming out of the water, they were vested and Chrismated. Next, he poured some wine into a wooden cup and mixed it with a portion of the presanctified Body of our Lord, which he had brought with him in a special container. He recited the Lord's Prayer, and then they received Holy Communion. The biographer of the three martyrs mentions that they lit candles and remained the entire day near that river "joyfully doxologizing God."

When these things happened, the Church was being severely persecuted. Nevertheless, far from the city, St. Loukianos continued the Apostolic Tradition. He baptized, chrismated and imparted Holy Communion to a group of people who chose to become followers of Jesus Christ.

PART THREE
POST BAPITSMAL PRAYERS

Prayers of the Washing

In ancient times, the washing of the newly illumined took place on the eighth day after Baptism. The practice of the Church, at that time, was for a person to wear their baptismal garment for eight days following their baptism. Each day, after the Gospel reading—unless the Divine Liturgy was not going to be celebrated—the Priest read the Prayers of Washing. In these prayers, the Priest entreats the Lord to: a) keep the newly baptized Christian safe from harm and to stand strong against every diabolical machination, b) to maintain his baptismal garment brilliant and unblemished, and c) to keep the spiritual Seal of the Holy Spirit unbroken.

The Priest takes a new water-filled sponge and washes the body of the neophyte in the places where he was anointed with Holy Chrism.

You have been baptized. You have been enlightened. You have been anointed with chrism. You have been sanctified. You have been washed clean. In the Name of the Father, and of the Son, and of the Holy Spirit. Amen.

The Celebrant is addressing him saying: My brother, you have been justified and enlightened with Holy Baptism. You have been anointed with Holy Chrism. You have been sanctified with Holy Communion. You have received all of these gifts in the name of the Father, and the Son, and the Holy Spirit!

The deeper meaning of the washing is this: the believer is reminded that he must be reverent with regard to the elements used for his spiritual regeneration. In other words, the water and myrrh—indeed, all the elements used at his Baptism, "which alone, and prior to their sanctification by the Holy Spirit, are of little value, but afterwards each of them takes on its own unique sanctifying power."

From the very beginning, the Church has taught the faithful to respect these elements. For example, in the case of infant Baptism, the mother is instructed to carefully save the rinse water after she bathes the child for the first time, and to pour it out at the side of the house, or in another place set apart. She is to do the same with the infant's baptismal clothes.

Prayers of the Tonsure

The Prayers of Tonsure mark the completion of the post-baptismal service. At this point, the Priest places his right hand on the neophyte's head and says: Lord our God...bless this *child / person* here present, and let Your blessing come down upon *his / her* head. As You blessed King David through Samuel the Prophet, bless too the head of Your servant *N.* through this sinful hand of mine, visiting *him / her* with Your Holy Spirit, so that as *he / she* advances to mature years and to the grey hairs of old age, *he / she* may give glory to You and see the good things of Jerusalem, all the days of *his / her* life.

This placement of the Priest's hand is the sign of blessing. It recalls how the Patriarch Jacob blessed his own descendants (Genesis 47:29–49:32), and how the Lord blessed the small children who came to Him (Mk. 10:13-16), and how when the Prophet Samuel blessed and anointed David, the Holy Spirit dwelt in him, making him a king. Now, the Priest entreats the all-Holy Spirit to descend upon the newly illumined person, now spiritually restored to his former glory.

When the Prayers of Tonsure are completed, the Priest cuts the hair of the person in a crosswise manner while saying: The servant of God *N.* is tonsured, in the Name of the Father, and of the Son, and of the Holy Spirit.

The tonsure signifies the dedication of a human being to God. Having received the divine blessings of Holy Baptism and Divine Chrismation—both priceless gifts—the newly illumined person responds in gratitude by offering himself to the source of these blessings, the Living God.

A Christian's first personal sacrifice to God is the offering of his hair. It is given in thanksgiving for the divine gift that he has received—new life in Christ!

TONSURE

Epilogue

One of the most beloved Saints of the twentieth century, St. Nektarios of Pentapolis, helps us to understand the significance and obligations that come with the gift of Holy Baptism. He writes,

"All of those who have been baptized in the name of Christ have been vested in Christ." (Gal. 3:27) These words of St. Paul are significant and true, and worthy of our consideration!

Baptized Christians ought not be dressed in the old man—with passions and sinful desires—but vested in the new man! Indeed, they have put on Christ, who has taken up an abode in their hearts! The expression, "put on", does not merely refer to some kind outer garment, but is something more profound, substantial and indelible.

We believe that at our Baptism, we were vested in Christ Himself, and thereby became children of God, dwelling places of the All-holy Spirit, divine temples, called to be perfect,

Saints and gods by grace. We cast off corruption and were clothed in incorruption. We were people of sin, but now of righteousness and grace. We were divested of death, and vested in immortality.

Have we understood the great responsibility that we have assumed before God on account of our Baptism?

Have we realized what sort of behavior is appropriate for children of God and brethren of our Lord, and that our will must align with God's will?

Do we understand that as His true children, we must remain free of sin, and that we must love Him with our whole heart?

Are we aware that He is due worship, and that we ought to yearn to be united with Him for all eternity?

I wonder if we have considered that our heart ought to be filled to overflowing with love, so that it spills over onto our fellow man?

Have we understood that we have been called to become holy and perfect, to be icons of God, His children and inheritors of the Kingdom of Heaven?

We must struggle for these things, so that we might be found worthy of the divine calling we have received, and not be rejected.

Yes, brethren, let none of us flag in zeal and be denied victory.

Let none of us lose our courage, nor be neglectful, faint-hearted, or intimidated in the face of spiritual struggle! For we have a God who will assist us and strengthen us as we struggle to acquire the virtues.

Blessed be those among us who have been vested in Christ, and not dirtied or wrinkled their shining baptismal garment. But, when we sin and pollute our soul, let us purify it with repentance and tears, so that with radiant souls, we might be found worthy of the Kingdom of Heaven.

Amen.

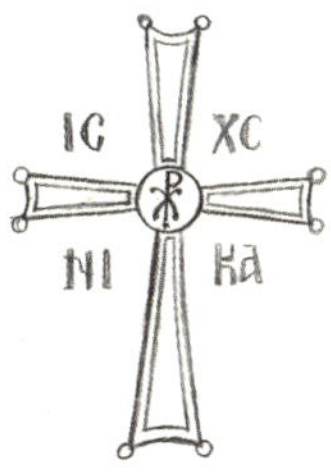

Necessary Items for the Celebration of the Mystery of Holy Baptism

The Godparent must provide the following new items:

⊕ One white baptismal garment (sticharion).

⊕ A large white towel

⊕ Two white hand cloths

⊕ A small container of pure olive oil

⊕ A baptismal cross (Note: the cross should be adult sized.)

⊕ Three candles for the baptismal font

⊕ One baptismal candle (NOTE: the baptismal candle should be an appropriate size, such that it can held by the Godparent while holding a child. It must also **only** have Christian symbols on it, such as a Cross or icon of the Lord, the Mother of God or the patron saint of the child.)

⊕ One bar of soap (NOTE: Ivory brand soap is preferable, because it floats and will not sink to the bottom of the baptismal font.)

⊕ Martyrika [witness pins]—small crosses or buttons that are worn by the attendees of the Holy Mystery, proclaiming their presence and joy at the reception of a new Christian into the Church of Christ.

ω
N

THE MYSTERY OF HOLY BAPTISM**

Pre-Baptismal Order

PRAYER FOR MAKING A CATECHUMEN

See p. 47

The Priest unties the girdle of the one who is about to be enlightened and divests them of outer clothing and shoes. He stands them facing East bareheaded and unshod, with the hands down. He breathes on their face three times, signs the forehead and chest three times, and places his hand on their head as he says the following Prayer:

In the Name of the Father, and the Son, and the Holy Spirit. Amen.

Blessed is our God, always, now, and forever, and to the ages of ages. Amen.

He places his hand on the candidate's head as he says the following Prayer:

Let us pray to the Lord.

** TRANSLATOR'S NOTE: This translation of the Mystery of Holy Baptism follows the order as it is celebrated in the Church of Greece. It is possible to see slight variations in the order of the Mystery to accommodate varying circumstances. This in no way changes the essential meaning of the Mystery.

In Your Name, Lord God of truth, and that of Your Only-Begotten Son, and Your Holy Spirit, I place my hand on the head of Your servant *N.*, who has been counted worthy to take refuge in Your holy Name and to be guarded under the shelter of Your wings. Remove from *him / her* that ancient error, and fill *him / her* with faith in You, and hope and love, so that *he / she* may know that You alone are God, true God, and Your Only-Begotten Son, our Lord Jesus Christ, and Your Holy Spirit. Grant that *he / she* may walk in Your commandments and preserve those things that are pleasing to You, for if someone does them, they will live by them. Inscribe *him / her* in Your book of life and unite *him / her* to the flock of Your inheritance. Let Your holy Name and that of Your beloved Son, our Lord Jesus Christ, and of Your life-giving Spirit, be glorified in *him / her*. Let Your eyes remain ever fixed in mercy on *him / her*, and Your ears to hear the voice of *his / her* supplication. Make *him / her* glad in the works of *his / her* hands and in all *his / her* Christian race, that *he / she* may confess You, worshipping and glorifying Your great and most high Name, and may praise You throughout all the days of *his / her* life.

See pp. 46–47

For every power of heaven sings Your praise, and Yours is the glory, of the Father, the Son, and the Holy Spirit, now and for ever, and to the ages of ages.

Choir: Amen.

FIRST EXORCISM

See p. 51

Deacon: Let us prayer to the Lord.

Choir: Lord, have mercy.

Priest:

The Lord rebukes you, O Devil, the Lord Who came into the world and dwelt among mankind so that He might destroy your tyranny and deliver humanity; the Lord Who on the Tree crushed the hostile powers when the sun was darkened, the earth shaken, the graves opened, and the bodies of the Saints arose; the Lord Who by death abolished death and destroyed the one who had the power of death, namely you, the Devil. I adjure you by the God Who revealed the Tree of Life and set in place the Cherubim and the flaming sword which turned this way and that to guard it: Be rebuked and withdraw! I adjure you by the One Who walked on the surface of the sea as on dry land and rebuked the tempest, the One Whose gaze dries up the deeps and whose curse melts mountains. For it is He who now commands you, through us: Be afraid, come out, withdraw from this creature and return no more. Do not hide in *him / her*, nor encounter *him / her*, nor influence *him / her* either by night or day, early or at noon. But go back to your own Tartarus until the Great Day of Judgement that has been prepared. Be afraid of God, Who is seated upon the Cherubim and looks upon the deeps; before Whom Angels, Archangels,

Thrones, Dominions, Principalities, Authorities, Powers, the many-eyed Cherubim and the six-winged Seraphim, tremble; before whom heaven and earth, the seas, and all that is in them tremble. Come out, and withdraw from the sealed and newly-enlisted soldier of Christ our God. For it is by Him that I adjure you, by the One Who walks on the wings of the winds, Who makes His Angels spirits and His ministers a flaming fire. Come out, and withdraw from this creature with all Your power and Your angels.

For the Name of the Father, and of the Son, and of the Holy Spirit has been glorified, now and for ever, and to the ages of ages.

Choir: Amen.

SECOND EXORCISM

Deacon: Let us pray to the Lord.

Choir: Lord, have mercy.

Priest:

It is God, the Holy One, Who is beyond understanding and unsearchable in all His works and in His strength, the One who foreordained for you, O Devil, the penalty of eternal damnation, that through us, his unprofitable servants, orders you, and every power that works with you, to depart from the one who has been newly sealed in the name of our Lord Jesus Christ, our true God. I adjure you, most evil, unclean, foul, abominable and alien spirit, by the power of Jesus Christ, Who has all authority in heaven and on earth, and Who said to the deaf and dumb demon, 'Come out of the man, and enter him no more!' Depart! Acknowledge the futility of your power, which had no authority even over swine. Remember the One Who ordered you, in accordance with your own request, to enter the herd of swine. Fear God, at whose command the earth was established upon the waters, Who created the heavens and fixed the mountains with a king post and the valleys with a cross-beam, placed sand as a boundary for the sea, and made a safe path through wild water; Who touches the mountains and they smoke; See p. 53 Who wraps Himself in light as in a garment, stretching out the heavens like a tent cloth; Who roofs His upper chambers with waters; Who established the earth on its foundations; it will not be moved from age to age; Who summoned the water of the sea and poured it out upon the face of the earth. Depart from the one who is being made ready for holy Enlightenment. I adjure you by the saving Passion of our Lord Jesus Christ, by His precious Body and Blood and His dread Coming; for He will come, and He will not delay, to judge the whole earth, and He will condemn you and the powers that work with you to the Gehenna of fire, handing you over to the exterior darkness, where the worm is unsleeping and the fire is not quenched.

For the might is Christ our God's, with the Father and the Holy Spirit, now and for ever, and to the ages of ages.

Choir: Amen.

THIRD EXORCISM

Deacon: Let us pray to the Lord.

Choir: Lord, have mercy.

Priest:

Lord Sabaoth, God of Israel, Who heal every disease and every sickness, look upon Your servant, search out, seek and drive from *him / her* all the activities of the Devil. Rebuke the unclean spirits and expel them, and cleanse the work of Your hands; and using Your swift force, crush Satan speedily under *his / her* feet and grant *him / her* victories against him and all his unclean spirits, so that, obtaining mercy from You, *he / she* may be found worthy of Your immortal and heavenly Mysteries and may give glory to You, the Father, the Son, and the Holy Spirit, now and for ever, and to the ages of ages.

Choir: Amen.

Deacon: Let us pray to the Lord.

Choir: Lord, have mercy.

Priest:

Master and Lord, the One Who Is, Who made man according to Your image and likeness and gave him the power of eternal life; then, when he fell through sin, You did not disdain him, but provided for the salvation of the world through the incarnation of Your Christ, do You Yourself receive also this creature of Yours, Whom You have redeemed from the slavery of the foe, into the heavenly Kingdom. Open the eyes of *his / her* mind so that the enlightenment of Your Gospel may dawn on *him / her*. Yoke to *his / her* life an Angel of light, to deliver *him / her* from every attack of the Adversary, from evil encounter, from the noon-day demon, and from evil visions.

See p. 54

And the Priest breathes on the mouth, forehead and chest, saying:

Drive out of *him / her* every evil and unclean spirit hiding and lurking in *his / her* heart. **(x3)**

The spirit of error, the spirit of wickedness, the spirit of idolatry and diabolic oppression; the spirit of lying and every uncleanness which operates in accordance with the teaching of the Devil. And make *him / her* a rational sheep of the flock of Your Christ, an honored member of Your Church, a vessel made holy, a *son / daughter* of light and an heir of Your Kingdom. So that, having lived in accordance with Your commandments, preserving the seal undamaged and keeping *his / her* garment undefiled, *he / she* may attain to the blessedness of the Saints in Your Kingdom.

By the grace and pity and love for mankind of Your Only-Begotten Son, with whom You are blessed, together with Your all-holy, good and life-giving Spirit, now and for ever, and to the ages of ages.

Choir: Amen.

When the Catechumen is undressed and unshod, the Priest turns him / her to the West with hands raised on high, and says:

See p. 57

Do you renounce Satan? And all his works? And all his angels? And all his worship? And all his solemn rites? *(x3)*

And to each question the Catechumen, or the Godparent (if the Catechumen is a young child, unable to communicate, or relies on an adult guardian), answers and says:

I renounce them. (x3)

And the Priest again asks the one to be baptized:

Have you renounced Satan? (x3)

And the Catechumen, or the Godparent, answers:

I have renounced him. (x3)

After he/she has said this three times the Priest says:

Then blow and spit on him.

After this the Priest turns the Catechumen to the East with lowered hands and says to him/her three times:

See p. 61

Do you unite yourself to Christ? (x3)

The Catechumen, or Godparent, answers three times:

I unite myself to Him. (x3)

And again the Priest asks three times:

Have you united yourself to Christ? (x3)

And each time the Catechumen, or Godparent, answers:

I have united myself to Him. (x3)

And the Priest asks:

And do you believe in Him?

The Catechumen, or Godparent, answers:

I believe in Him as King and God.

SYMBOL OF FAITH

See p. 62

I believe in one God, Father Almighty, Creator of heaven and earth and of all things visible and invisible.

And in one Lord Jesus Christ, the only-begotten Son of God, begotten of the Father before all ages. Light of Light, true God of true God, begotten not created, of one essence with the Father, through Whom all things were made.

Who for us men and for our salvation came down from heaven, and was incarnate of the Holy Spirit and the Virgin Mary, and became man.

He was crucified for us under Pontius Pilate. He suffered and was buried.

And He rose on the third day, according to the Scriptures.

He ascended into heaven and is seated at the right hand of the Father.

And He will come again with glory to judge the living and dead. His kingdom shall have no end.

And in the Holy Spirit, the Lord, the Creator of life, Who proceeds from the Father, Who together with the Father and the Son is worshipped and glorified, Who spoke through the prophets.

In one, holy, catholic, and apostolic Church.

I confess one Baptism for the forgiveness of sins.

I look for the Resurrection of the dead and the life of the age to come. Amen. **(x3)**

When the holy Profession of Faith has been completed, the Priest again asks three times: Have you united yourself to Christ? *and the rest. The Catechumen, or the Godparent, answers each time as before. After the third question and the third recitation of the Creed, the Priest asks three times:*

Have you united yourself to Christ? **(x3)**

And the Catechumen, or the Godparent, answers:

I have united myself to Him.

And the Priest says:

Bow down also and worship Him.

The candidate makes a prostration, saying:

I worship Father, Son, and Holy Spirit, the Trinity consubstantial and undivided.

The Priest says:

Blessed is God Who wishes all to be saved and come to the knowledge of the truth, now and for ever, and to the ages of ages.

Choir: Amen.

Then he says this Prayer:

Deacon: Let us pray to the Lord.

Choir: Lord, have mercy.

Priest:

Master, Lord our God, call Your servant *N.* to Your holy Enlightenment, and count *him / her* worthy of the great grace of Your Holy Baptism. Put off *his / her* old self and renew *him / her* for eternal life and fill *him / her* with the power of Your Holy Spirit for union with Your Christ, that *he / she* may no longer be a child of the body, but a child of Your Kingdom.

Through the good pleasure and grace of Your Only-begotten Son, with Whom You are blessed, together with Your all-holy, good, and life-giving Spirit, now and for ever, and to the ages of ages.

Choir: Amen.

Dismissal.

Priest: Glory to You, O God, our hope, glory to You.

Reader: Glory to the Father, and the Son, and the Holy

Spirit. Both now and ever and to the ages of ages. Amen. Lord have mercy. **(x3)** Holy Father, bless.

Priest:

May Christ our true God *(who rose from the dead)*, as a good, loving, and merciful God, have mercy upon us and save us, through the intercessions of His most pure and holy Mother; the power of the precious and life giving Cross; the protection of the honorable, bodiless powers of heaven, the supplications of the honorable, glorious prophet and forerunner John the Baptist; the holy, glorious and praiseworthy Apostles; the holy, glorious and triumphant Martyrs; our holy and God-bearing Fathers *(name of the church)*; the holy and righteous ancestors of God, Joachim and Anna; Saint *(of the day)* whose memory we commemorate today, and all the Saints.

Priest: Through the prayers of our Holy Fathers, Lord Jesus Christ, our God, have mercy on us and save us.

Choir: Amen.

THE SERVICE OF HOLY BAPTISM

See p. 65

The Priest enters the Sanctuary and vests in white vestments and the cuffs. While all the candles are being lit, he takes the censer, goes to the Font, and censes it in a circle. He hands the censer away and makes a bow.

Then the Deacon says:

Master, give the blessing.

The Priest, out loud:

See p. 66

Blessed is the Kingdom of the Father, and of the Son, and of the Holy Spirit, now and for ever, and to the ages of ages.

Choir: Amen.

Deacon: In peace let us pray to the Lord.

Choir: Lord, have mercy. *(And so after each petition.)*

Deacon: For the peace from above and the salvation of our souls, let us pray to the Lord.

For peace in the whole world, for the stability of the holy Churches of God, and for the unity of all, let us pray to the Lord.

For this holy house and for those who enter it with faith, reverence, and the fear of God, let us pray to the Lord.

For our Archbishop *(Name)*, for the honored order of Presbyters, for the Diaconate in Christ, for all the clergy and the people, let us pray to the Lord.

That this water may be sanctified by the power, operation and descent of the Holy Spirit, let us pray to the Lord.

That there may be sent down upon it the grace of redemption and the blessing of Jordan, let us pray to the Lord.

That there may come down upon these waters the cleansing operation of the Trinity beyond being, let us pray to the Lord.

That we may be enlightened with the enlightenment of knowledge and true religion through the descent of the Holy Spirit, let us pray to the Lord.

That this water may be shown to be a protection against every assault of visible and invisible enemies, let us pray to the Lord.

That the one to be baptized in it may become worthy of the incorruptible Kingdom, let us pray to the Lord.

For the one who now draws near for holy Enlightenment, and for *his / her* safety and salvation, let us pray to the Lord.

That *he / she* may be shown to be a *son / daughter* of light and heir of eternal blessings, let us pray to the Lord.

That *he / she* may be rooted in, and be a partaker in, the death and resurrection of Christ our God, let us pray to the Lord.

That *he / she* may preserve the garment of Baptism and the pledge of the Holy Spirit unsullied and undefiled on the dread Day of Christ our God, let us pray to the Lord.

That this water may become for *him / her* a washing of rebirth for forgiveness of sins and a garment of incorruption, let us pray to the Lord.

That the Lord God would hearken to the voice of our supplication, let us pray to the Lord.

For our deliverance from all affliction, wrath, danger, and distress, let us pray to the Lord.

Take hold of us, save us, have mercy upon us, and protect us, O God, by Your grace.

Choir: Lord, have mercy.

Deacon: Commemorating our most holy, most pure, most blessed and glorified Lady the Theotokos and ever-virgin Mary, together with all the Saints, let us commit ourselves and one another and all our life unto Christ our God.

Choir: To You, O Lord.

While the Deacon is saying this the Priest says this prayer quietly:

Compassionate and merciful God, You test minds and hearts and alone know the secrets of mortals, for no deed is hidden in Your sight, but everything is naked and exposed to Your eyes. You know all about me; do not then despise me or turn Your face from me, but overlook my offences at this hour, You who overlook the sins of mortals for their repentance. Wash away the filth of my body and the defilement of my soul by the power of Your invisible and spiritual right hand, lest, as I proclaim freedom to others and grant it by the perfect faith of Your ineffable love for mankind, I myself, as a slave of sin, become unworthy of it. Master, alone good and lover of mankind, may I not be turned away humiliated and put to shame, but from on high, send power out to me and give me strength for Your great and heavenly Mystery which lies before me, and through my miserable person, form Your Christ in the one who is about to be reborn. Build *him / her* up on the foundation of Your Apostles and Prophets, and do not pull *him / her* down, but plant *him / her* as a plant of truth in Your holy Catholic and Apostolic Church, and do not pull *him / her* out. So that by *his / her* progressing in true religion, Your all-holy Name, of Father, Son, and Holy Spirit, may be glorified also through *him / her*, now and for ever, and to the ages of ages. Amen.

It is to be noted that the Priest says none of this out loud, but he even says the Amen *to himself.*

Then he says the following prayer in a loud voice:

Great are You, O Lord, and wonderful are Your works; and no word will be adequate to sing the praise of Your wonders. **(x3)** See p. 67

For as by Your will, You brought the universe from non-existence into being, by Your might You uphold creation, and by Your providence You direct the world. From four elements, You composed the world, with four seasons You crowned the circle of the year. All the spiritual Powers tremble before You. The sun sings Your praises, the moon glorifies You, the stars entreat You, the light obeys You, the deeps tremble before You, and the springs are Your servants. You stretched out the heavens like a curtain; You established the earth on the waters; You walled-in the sea with sand; You poured out the air for breathing. Angelic Powers minister to You, the choirs of Archangels worship You, the many-eyed Cherubim and the six-winged Seraphim, as they stand and fly around You, veiling themselves in fear of Your unapproachable glory. For You, God uncircumscribed, without beginning and ineffable, came upon earth, taking the form of a slave, being found in the likeness of mortals. For through the compassion of Your mercy, Master, You could not endure to watch the human race being tyrannized by the Devil, but You came and saved us. We confess Your grace, we proclaim Your mercy, we do not conceal Your benevolence. You set at liberty the generations of our human nature, You sanctified a virgin womb by Your birth. All creation sang Your praise when You appeared. For You, our God, were seen on earth and lived among mankind. You also sanctified the streams of the Jordan by sending upon them Your All-holy Spirit from Heaven, and You crushed the heads of the dragons that lurked there in the waters.

Therefore, O King, Lover of mankind, be present now too, through the visitation of Your Holy Spirit, and sanc-
See p. 69
tify this water **(x3)**.

Give it the grace of redemption, the blessing of the Jordan. Make it a source of incorruption, a gift of sanctification, a deliverance from sins, a destruction of demons. Make it unapproachable by hostile powers and filled with angelic strength. Let those that conspire against Your creature flee from it, because I, Lord, have called upon Your Name, which is wondrous and glorious and fearful to adversaries.

And sealing the water
and breathing on it three times, he prays saying:

Let all adverse powers be crushed beneath the sign of
See p. 70
the image of Your Cross. **(x3)**

We pray You, Lord, let all airy and invisible spectres withdraw from us, and do not let a demon of darkness hide itself in this water, and do not let an evil spirit, bringing darkening of thoughts and disturbance of mind, go down into it with the one who is being baptized. But do

You, Master of all things, declare this water to be water of redemption, water of sanctification, cleansing of flesh and spirit, untying of bonds, forgiveness of offences, enlightenment of soul, washing of rebirth, renewal of spirit, gift of adoption, garment of incorruption, and source of life. For it was You, Lord, who said, 'Wash and be made clean, and put away evils from your souls'. It is You who have given us the grace of rebirth from on high through water and Spirit. Manifest Yourself, Lord, in this water, and grant that the one being baptized in it may be transformed for the putting off of the old self that is corrupted by the desires of deception, and may put on the new self that is renewed after the image of the One who created *him / her*. So that, planted in the likeness of Your death through Baptism, *he / she* may also become a partaker in Your Resurrection, and having guarded the gift of the Holy Spirit and increased the deposit of grace, may receive the prize of *his / her* high calling and be numbered with the firstborn, whose names are inscribed in heaven, in You, our God and Lord, Jesus Christ. See p. 71

For to You belong glory, might, honor and worship, together with Your Father who is without beginning, and Your all-holy, good, and life-giving Spirit, now and for ever, and to the ages of ages.

Choir: Amen.

Priest: Peace to all.

Choir: And to your spirit.

Deacon: Let us bow our heads to the Lord.

Choir: To You, O Lord.

The Priest breathes on the container of oil three times and signs the oil three times as it held by the Deacon (or Godparent).

Deacon: Let us pray to the Lord.

Choir: Lord, have mercy.

See p. 74–73

The Priest say the following Prayer quietly:

Master, Lord God of our Fathers, Who sent out a dove to those in Noah's ark, with a branch of olive in its beak as a sign of reconciliation and salvation from the Flood, and through these things prefigured the Mystery of Grace; who have given the fruit of the olive for the completion of Your holy Mysteries; who through it both filled those under the Law with the Holy Spirit, and made perfect those under grace; do You Yourself bless this olive oil also by the power, operation and descent of Your Holy Spirit, so that it may become an anointing of incorruption, a weapon of righteousness, renewal of soul and body, a repellent of every operation of the Devil, for the removal of all evils from those who are anointed with it in faith, or who partake of it to Your glory, and that of Your Only-Begotten Son, and Your all-holy, good, and life-giving Spirit, now and for ever, and to the ages of ages.

Choir: Amen.

Deacon: Let us attend.

The Priest, chanting Alleluia *three times with the people, makes three Crosses with the oil in the water. Then he proclaims:*

Blessed is God, Who enlightens and sanctifies everyone who comes into the world, now and for ever, and to the ages of ages. See p. 76

Choir: Amen.

The one to be baptized is brought forward. The Priest takes some of the oil and makes the sign of the Cross on the forehead, chest and back of the candidate, saying:

The servant of God, *N.*, is anointed with the oil of gladness, in the Name of the Father, and of the Son, and of the Holy Spirit. Amen. See p. 76–76

As he signs their chest and back he says:

For healing of soul and body.

On the ears:

For the hearing of faith.

On the feet:

For your feet to walk.

On the hands:

Your hands made me and fashioned me.

And when the whole body has been anointed, the Priest baptizes the person, holding them upright and facing East, as he says:

The servant of God *N.* is baptized, in the Name of the Father. Amen. And of the Son. Amen. And of the Holy Spirit. Amen. See p. 79

At each invocation the Priest immerses them and raises them again. After the baptism the Priest washes, as he and the people chant (x3):

See p. 84

Psalm 31

Blessed are those whose iniquities have been forgiven and whose sins have been covered. **(x3)**

Reader: Blessed is the man to whom the Lord imputes no sin and in whose mouth there is no guile. Because I kept silent, my bones grew old from my crying out all day long. Because night and day your hand was heavy upon me; I was turned to wretchedness by a thorn being fastened in me. I acknowledged my sin and did not hide my iniquity. I said, 'Against myself I will admit my iniquity to the Lord', and You forgave the ungodliness of my heart. For this, every holy one will pray to You at a fitting moment. Except in a flood of many waters, they will not come near him. For You are my refuge from the affliction which surrounds me, my joy to deliver me from those who have surrounded me. 'I will make you understand and guide you in the way in which you should go. I will fix my eyes upon you. Do not become like horse and mule, who have no understanding. With bit and bridle you must constrain their cheeks so that they do not come near you.' Many are the scourges of the sinner, but mercy will surround the one who hopes in the Lord. Rejoice in the Lord and be glad you righteous, and boast all you upright in heart.

Deacon: Let us pray to the Lord.

Choir: Lord, have mercy.

And the Priest says this prayer:

Blessed are You, Lord God Almighty, the source of blessings, the Sun of righteousness, who have made the light of salvation shine for those in darkness through the appearing of Your Only-Begotten Son and our God, and have granted us, unworthy though we are, the grace of blessed cleansing by Holy Baptism, and divine sanctification by life-giving Anointing. And You have now been well-pleased to make Your newly-enlightened servant to be born again through water and Spirit, and have granted *him / her* forgiveness of sins, both voluntary and involuntary. Do You then, Master, compassionate, universal King, grant *him / her* also the Seal of the gift of Your of all-powerful Holy Spirit, Who is worthy of all honor and worship, and the Communion of the holy Body and precious Blood of Your Christ. Keep *him / her* in Your sanctification; confirm *him / her* in the Orthodox Faith; deliver *him / her* from the Evil One and all his devices, and by Your saving fear guard *his / her* soul in purity and righteousness; so that being in every deed and word well-pleasing to You, *he / she* may become a *son / daughter* and heir of Your heavenly Kingdom.

See p. 89

Aloud:

For You are our God, a God who has mercy and who saves, and to You we give glory, to the Father, and to the Son, and to the Holy Spirit, now and for ever, and to the ages of ages.

Choir: Amen.

And after the prayer he anoints the newly baptized with the holy Myron, making a sign of the Cross on the forehead, the eyes, the nostrils, the mouth, the two ears, the chest, the hands and the feet, and saying:

See p. 94–93 The Seal of the gift of the Holy Spirit. Amen.

And as he clothes the newly baptized, the Priest says:

See p. 97 The servant of God *N.* is clothed with a garment of righteousness, in the Name of the Father, and of the Son, and of the Holy Spirit. Amen.

Then the following is chanted in Tone Pl. 4.

Grant me a tunic of light, O most merciful, Christ our God, Who wrap Yourself in light as in a garment.

Then the Priest, having washed his hands, censes the Font, going round it in a circle, with the Godparent and the Newly-baptized following and standing opposite him, while we chant:

See p. 104–103 All those who have been baptized into Christ have put on Christ. Alleluia. **(x3)**

Glory to the Father, and to the Son, and to the Holy Spirit. Both now and for ever, and to the ages of ages. Amen.

Have put on Christ. Alleluia.

Deacon: With strength.

All those who have been baptized into Christ have put on Christ. Alleluia.

Deacon: Let us attend.

Reader: The Lord is my enlightenment and my Saviour; * whom shall I fear?

Verse: The Lord is the defender of my life, of whom shall I be afraid?

Deacon: Wisdom.

Reader: The Reading is from the Epistle of Paul to the Romans. See p. 106

Deacon: Let us attend.

Reader:

(6:3-11)

Brethren, do you not know that all we who were baptized into Christ Jesus were baptized into His death? And so, we were buried with Him through baptism to death, so that just as Christ was raised from the dead by the glory of the Father, [likewise] we might also walk in newness of life. Truly, if we have become united with Him in the likeness of His death, we will also be [united with Him] by a Resurrection like His. It means that we recognize this, that our old humanity was crucified with Him, so that the body of sin might be done away with, and so that we would no longer be in bondage to sin. Whoever has died has been freed from sin! But if we have died with Christ, we believe that we will also live with Him; knowing that Christ, being raised from the dead, dies no more. Death no longer has dominion over Him! For the death that He died, He died to sin one time; but the life that He lives, He lives to God. Thus, consider yourselves to be dead as regards sin, but alive to God in Christ Jesus our Lord.

Priest: Peace to you.

Reader: And to your spirit. Alleluia, Alleluia, Alleluia.

Deacon: Wisdom. Arise. Let us hear the Holy Gospel.

Priest: Peace to all.

Choir: And to your spirit.

See p. 107

Priest: The Reading is from the holy Gospel according to Matthew.

Choir: Glory to You, O Lord, glory to You.

Deacon: Let us attend.

Priest:

(28:16-20)

At that time, the eleven disciples went into Galilee, to the mountain where Jesus had directed them. When they saw Him, they expressed adoration to Him, but they doubted. Jesus came to them and said, "All authority has been given to me in heaven and on earth. Go therefore and make disciples of all nations, baptizing them in the Name of the Father and of the Son and of the Holy Spirit, teaching them to observe all the things that I have commanded you. Behold, I am with you always, even to the end of the age." Amen!

Choir: Glory to You, O Lord, glory to You.

Then the Litany and Dismissal. [Note: Frequently the Ablution and Tonsure are done before the Litany.]

Deacon: Have mercy on us, O God, according to Your great mercy, we pray You, hear and have mercy.

Choir: Lord, have mercy. **(x3)**

Deacon: Again we pray for mercy, life, peace, health, salvation and forgiveness of sins, for the servants, the newly enlightened *N.*, *his/her* Sponsor *N.*, and all those people who are present.

Again we pray for the newly enlightened servant of God *N.*

Priest: For You, O God, are good and love mankind, and to You we give glory, to the Father and to the Son and to the Holy Spirit, now and for ever, and to the ages of ages.

Choir: Amen.

Deacon: Let us pray to the Lord.

Choir: Lord, have mercy.

See p. 113

PRAYERS OF THE WASHING

Priest:

Master and Lord, who have granted Your servant forgiveness of sins through Holy Baptism, and given *him / her* the grace of a life of rebirth, be well pleased for the illumination of Your face to shine for ever in *his / her* heart; keep the shield of *his / her* faith safe from attack by foes; preserve on *him / her* the garment of incorruption, which *he / she* has put on, undefiled and unstained; by Your grace keeping the spiritual seal unbroken in *him / her*, and being merciful to *him / her* and to us.

For blessed and glorified is Your all-honored and majestic Name, of the Father, the Son, and the Holy Spirit, now and for ever, and to the ages of ages.

Choir: Amen.

Deacon: Let us pray to the Lord.

Choir: Lord, have mercy.

Priest:

Master, Lord our God, who through the font grant heavenly radiance to those who are baptized, who have given Your newly enlightened servant rebirth through water and Spirit, and granted *him / her* forgiveness of sins both voluntary and involuntary, lay Your mighty hand on *him / her* and guard *him / her* by the power of Your loving kindness; preserve the pledge inviolate; and count *him / her* worthy of eternal life and Your good pleasure.

Because You are our sanctification, and to You we give glory, to the Father, the Son, and the Holy Spirit, now and for ever, and to the ages of ages.

Choir: Amen.

Priest: Peace to all.

Choir: And to your spirit.

Deacon: Let us bow our heads to the Lord.

Choir: To You, O Lord.

Priest:

The one who has put You on, Christ our God, has bowed *his / her* head to You with us. Guard *him / her* always to remain an invincible warrior against those that in vain bear enmity against *him / her* and us, and with Your incorruptible crown, declare us all to be victors unto the end.

For Yours it is to have mercy and to save us, and to You we give glory, with Your Father who is without beginning, and Your all-holy, good and life-giving Spirit, now and for ever, and to the ages of ages.

Choir: Amen.

And he unties the girdle and linen cloth of the newly baptized, and having joined their ends, he wets them with water and sprinkles the newly baptized, saying:

Priest: You have been justified. You have been enlightened.

And taking a new sponge with water, he sponges the face of the newly baptized, together with their head, chest and the rest, saying:

Priest: You have been baptized. You have been enlightened. You have been anointed with chrism. You have been sanctified. You have been washed clean. In the Name of the Father, and of the Son, and of the Holy Spirit. Amen.

See p. 115

PRAYERS FOR THE TONSURE

Deacon: Let us pray to the Lord.

Choir: Lord, have mercy.

Priest:

Master, Lord our God, who honored mortals with Your image, furnishing them with a rational soul and a comely body, so that the body might serve the rational soul, You placed the head at the very top, and in it You planted the majority of the senses, which do not interfere with one another, while You covered the head with hair so as not to be harmed by the changes of the weather, and You fitted all the limbs most suitably to each one, so that through them all, they might give thanks to You the Master Craftsman. Do You Yourself,

Master, who through Your vessel of election, the Apostle Paul, ordered us to do all things to Your glory, bless Your servant *N.* who has come to make a first offering by the cutting of the hair of *his / her* head. Bless *his / her* Sponsor also, and grant that *he / she* may always meditate on Your law and do what is well-pleasing to You.

For You, O God, are merciful and love mankind, and to You we give glory, to the Father and to the Son and to the Holy Spirit, now and for ever, and to the ages of ages.

Choir: Amen.

Priest: Peace to all.

Choir: And to your spirit.

Deacon: Let us bow our heads to the Lord.

Choir: To You, O Lord.

Deacon: Let us pray to the Lord.

Choir: Lord, have mercy.

Priest:

Lord our God, who through Your loving kindness have sanctified from the fullness of the font those who believe in You, bless this *child / person* here present, and let Your blessing come down upon *his / her* head. As You blessed King David through Samuel the Prophet, bless too the head of Your servant *N.* through this sinful hand of mine, visiting *him / her* with Your Holy Spirit, so that as *he / she* advances to mature years and to the grey hairs of old age, *he / she* may give glory to You and see the good things of Jerusalem, all the days of *his / her* life.

For to You belong all glory, honor and worship, to the Father and to the Son and to the Holy Spirit, now and for ever, and to the ages of ages.

Choir: Amen.

And the Priest tonsures them in the form of a cross, saying:

The servant of God *N.* is tonsured, in the Name of the Father, and of the Son, and of the Holy Spirit.

Choir: Amen.

Deacon: Have mercy on us, O God, according to Your great mercy, we pray You, hear and have mercy.

Choir: Lord, have mercy. **(x3)**

Again we pray for mercy, life, peace, health, salvation and forgiveness of sins for the servants, the newly enlightened *N.*, *his / her* Sponsor *N.*, and all those people who are present.

Priest: For You, O God, are merciful and love mankind, and to You we give glory, to the Father, the Son, and the Holy Spirit, now and for ever, and to the ages of ages.

Choir: Amen.

And the Dismissal

Priest: Glory to You, O God, our hope, glory to You.

Reader: Glory to the Father, and to the Son, and to the

Holy Spirit, both now and for ever, and to the ages of ages. Amen.

Lord, have mercy. Lord, have mercy. Lord, have mercy.

Holy Father, give the blessing.

Priest:

May He who deigned to be baptized by John in the Jordan, Christ our true God, through the prayers of His all-pure and holy Mother, through the intercessions of the honored, glorious Prophet, Forerunner and Baptist, John, of the holy, glorious and all-praised Apostles, of the holy and righteous ancestors of God, Joachim and Anna, of Saint *N. (the Saint of the Newly-baptized)*, of Saint *N. (to whom the Church is dedicated)*, of Saint *N.*, whose memory we keep today, and of all the Saints, have mercy on us and save us, for He is good and loves mankind.

Through the prayers of our Holy Fathers, Lord Jesus Christ, our God, have mercy on us and save us.

Choir: Amen.

Note: *It is customary that, while the Priest washes following the Baptism and Christmation of a Child, the Katavasias of the Resurrection to be sung from Bright Week until the Leave-taking of Pascha, and the Katavasias of the Exaltation of the Precious Cross during the rest of the year.*

IC
NI
KA
XP

GLOSSARY

A

Adherence

...is the attachment or commitment to a person, cause, or belief.

Aitolian

... is a person from Aitolia, a mountainous region of Greece on the north coast of the Gulf of Corinth.

Alexandria

... is an important city in Egypt, founded in 332 BC by Alexander the Great. According to the Church's Tradition, the Apostle and Evangelist Mark is considered to be the Founder and first Bishop of the Alexandrian Church. Saint Mark arrived in Alexandria in AD 43, the same year in which he founded the Alexandrian Church.

Alleluia

...Hebrew word that means 'Praise God.'

Amen

...is a Hebrew word which is translated in various ways: *So be it*; *Truly*; *Indeed*. When someone says the word *Amen* in response to a statement, that person proclaims their assent to what has been said. Amen is also said at the conclusion of prayers.

Antioch

...was an ancient city founded near the end of the fourth century BC by Seleucus I Nicator, one of Alexander the Great's generals. It was in the city of Antioch (modern day Antakya in southeast Turkey) that Christians were first so called (Acts 11:26). According to the Church's Tradition, Saint Peter established the Church in Antioch.

B

Baptismal Candidate

...is a person who is being prepared for Baptism, i.e., to receive the light of Christ and to be liberated from the darkness of error.

Beautiful Gate

...is the central doorway in front of the Sanctuary, which is closed by double gates and a curtain, and is used only by the clergy.

Boldness

...is confidence of presence and expression in relationship to another person. In Paradise, Adam saw the face of God with boldness. The Saints possess authentic boldness, and this allows them to intercede to God for us.

C

Canonical [canonically]

...is whatever has been done in accordance with the Canons of the Church, and is therefore valid. (A canonical ordination must follow the prescriptions of the 1st and 2nd Canons of the Apostolic Constitutions.)

Catechumen

...is a person who has expressed a desire to be baptized and become a member of the Church. Prior to their Baptism, a Catechumen must be instructed in the faith. This instruction is called catechesis.

Catechumenate

...is the period of religious and moral instruction, prior to Holy Bpatism.

Circumcision

...is a Jewish rite for baby boys, the purpose of which was to integrate the child into the community of faith. The Jews practiced this rite on the eighth day after birth.

Communion, Holy

...is one of the seven Mysteries of the Church during which bread and wine are transformed into the Body and Blood of Christ. This Mystery was established at the Mystical Supper.

E

Eunuch

...a castrated man who has been employed to guard the women's living areas at an oriental court.

F

Forerunner

...is a person whose life and activity prepares for the work of someone else.

Foreshadow

...is an indication of a person or future event through images and symbols.

I

Incarnation

...is the assumption of human nature (enfleshment) by Jesus Christ.

M

Mime

...is the theatrical technique of suggesting action, character, or emotion without words, using only gesture, expression, and movement.

Myrrh, Holy [also called Chrism]

...is sanctified oil that is made with forty fragrant essences (which symbolize the gifts of the Holy Spirit), which is sanctified on Holy Thursday at the Patriarchal Church in Constantinople by the Patriarch at a special service. Following its preparation, the myrrh is distributed to all the Orthodox Churches throughout the world. This is the oil that is used to anoint the neophyte during the Mystery of Holy Chrismation.

P

Comforter

...is another name for the Holy Spirit.

Pericope

...is a selection from one of the books of the Old Testament, the Letters, the Acts of the Apostles, or the Divine Gospel, which is read during the divine services of the Church.

Presbyter [Priest]

...is a clergyman of the Church who holds the second of three degrees of the priesthood. (the other two being Deacon and Bishop).

S

Sanctuary

...(in Greek, literally the Holy Step, because it is elevated from the rest of the Temple by a series of steps) is the most sacred part of the Temple, and is separated from the Nave by the Icon Screen. It symbolizes Heaven, where the divine Throne is found. The Sanctuary is always at the east end of the Temple. Various other names are used to describe this part of the Church, including the Sacred Place, the Holy of Holies, and the Inner Sanctum.

Spiritual Meadow [Leimonarion]

...is a book of monastic origin that contains a collection of teachings and the virtuous deeds of the Saints, Martyrs, and Monastics. The *Evergetinos* and *Gerontikon* are similar collections.

T

Tonsure

...is **a)** the rite of monastic tonsure, **b)** to cut the hair.

Tonsure, Monastic

...is the rite where a layperson enters the monastic rank by tonsure. In this service the person's hair is cut in a cruciform manner, as an indication of their total devotion to God.